ROBERTS RULES!

Success Secrets from America's Most Trusted Sports Agent

By
Marc Roberts
with
Theresa Foy DiGeronimo

CAREER
PRESS

ROBERTS RULES!
Cover design by Rossman Design
Printed in the U.S.A. by Book-mart Press

To order this title, please call toll-free 1-800-CAREER-1 (NJ and Canada: 201-848-0310) to order using VISA or MasterCard, or for further information on books from Career Press.

Library of Congress Cataloging-in-Publication Data

Roberts, Marc.
    Roberts rules! : success secrets from America's most trusted
sports agent / by Marc Roberts with Theresa DiGeronimo.
       p.   cm.
    Includes index.
    ISBN 1-56414-371-6 (hardcover)
    1. Sports agents.   2. Roberts, Marc.   I. DiGeronimo, Theresa Foy.
II. Title.
GV734.5.R63   1998
796'.06'9--dc21   98-28107

Dedication

I'd like to dedicate this book to the following people who have been instrumental in making me what I am today:

My parents, Roz and Roy, who gave me the best childhood ever, always gave me the freedom when I was growing up to develop my own personality, and always tried to support me. I love you both.

My dad is also executive officer of Worldwide Entertainment and Sports. Just knowing he's running things let's me get out and be my best without worrying about things.

My grandmother, Bertha Goff, "Ma." Thank God I have inherited her incredible business acumen. Thank you for always loving me so much—you're the most wonderful "Ma" any kid could have. I love you.

My grandmother, Nanny Rabinowitz, who I loved with all my heart for being a tremendous grandmother. I miss her every day.

My brother Dave and his lovely wife, Pat, one of the happiest couples I know, and two of my biggest supporters.

My brother Barry and his beautiful wife, Patti, both brilliant businesspeople and the best parents of all time.

Robert Schultz, my unbelievable cousin, who is a best friend and big brother to me. He has always been there for me and I appreciate his support more than he will ever know.

Barry Farber, my literary agent and childhood friend. Without his vision, hard work, energy, and enthusiasm, this book would not exist. From one agent to another, Barry, you are the best in the world.

Herb Kozlov, the best attorney in the world and a great partner in WWES. Thanks for letting me bounce ideas off you and for being incredibly loyal and committed to my vision. You have never let me down. I look forward to being with you forever.

Harvey Silverman, my mentor. If it weren't for Harvey, there would be nothing to write about in this book, because Worldwide Entertainment and Sports would not exist. In every successful person's life, there is one special person who can be credited with making the difference—in my life, Harvey Silverman is that person.

Irwin Gold, an outstanding businessman and a super cousin, who is also one of my best friends. Thanks for being so supportive.

Greg Cohen, my cousin, who is a younger brother to me and who at a young age, is a boxing veteran, and his beautiful wife, Michele, who is one of the top commodities traders in the world.

Joe Marino, for being there for me in the embryonic stages of WWES. Thanks for all the great times.

Joe Gamberale, for his unbelievable introductions that led to some historic events and fierce loyalty.

Alexander P. Cohen, my adorable godson, means the world to me.

Ali and Cari Roberts, my beautiful nieces, who I will always keep close to my heart and for whom I will always be there. I love you so much. No uncle has ever been more proud of his nieces.

Alan Cohen, my uncle, who, especially in the early years, gave and continues to give me much needed support and encouragement. I'll never forget that he was always there for me; to this day, he is one of my chief advisors on my board of directors.

Aunt Jill Cohen, my godmother, a first-class woman and the world's best CPA.

Sherry and David Shapiro, great lawyers and my genius cousins.

Corey and Samantha Shapiro, my cute cousins, both of whom are future geniuses.

Kenny Greene, a great friend who is always there to listen. At a young age, he has accomplished a lot and will accomplish much more in the future. I consider him to be like a brother.

Judy Feit, my gorgeous cousin for whom I'll always be there.

Gary "Hap" Hollander, a true best friend who had the vision to believe in me when others didn't. He will always be well-rewarded for that. He has always been fiercely loyal to me and never lets me down. He is an integral part of Worldwide Entertainment and Sports.

Shannon Briggs, whom I am so proud of for coming so far; he is the only son I will ever have. He will be the Heavyweight Champion of the World. I have instilled in him my strong belief in the value of networking and the importance of the words *hard work*, *loyalty*, and *determination*. We will always be there for one another.

Mitchell Modell, president of Modell's Sporting Goods. A great friend, businessman, and networker whom I learn so much from just through osmosis. He will be one of my best friends forever.

Rich Rubenstein, one of my best friends in the world. He is the best at what he does in an area of expertise that helps me and my business. He would do anything for me and I would do anything for him. He is a true friend with whom I will go the distance.

Alyssa Held, the most gorgeous and brilliant lawyer who's always been there for me and who I'll always love. Thanks for all your support when I needed it most.

Terry Rucker and his beautiful wife, Debbie. I love them both. Ruck, no one could ask for a better best friend. Thanks for all the amazing times.

Jay Levy, my best friend and true sparring partner. No matter what happens to me, good or bad, I know there is one person who will always be there for me, who I can trust, and who will never let me down. That person is my best friend, Mr. Jay "LaBalBo" Levy.

Peter Levy, my best friend, brother, and genius who believes in me so much. I can't begin to tell him how much I appreciate his loyalty and friendship. I can count on Peter for anything and I am very lucky to have met him.

Peter Ziering, one of my best friends and a loyal supporter who shares my vision. He will do anything to help me accomplish my goals. I appreciate that he drops everything when I need him to do something for me. His help is invaluable.

Jeff Goldstern and his wife, Jessica, the "Goldies," two of my best friends who have always been there for me and who would do anything to help me succeed. Jeff is unbelievably loyal to me and I trust him as much as I trust anyone. Jessica is one of my all-time favorites.

Marty Bell, one of my best friends who always tried to help me and who gave me access to his terrific Rolodex.

Theresa Foy DiGeronimo is the Babe Ruth of collaborators. Her ability to pull out of me the stories of my business life and shape them into compelling lessons makes this book come alive.

Acknowledgments

There are many people in my life who have been there for me when it mattered and who have made it possible for me to be successful in my field. I would like to acknowledge:

Rich Abramson, Bob Arum, Bruce Beck, Ken Berman, Lisa Boomhower, Russell "Boo" Bowers, Rich Bronson, Arnie Budin, Mike Cantor, Ron Cantor, Career Press staff (Anne Brooks, Stacey A. Farkas, Michael Gaffney, Betsy Sheldon), Joe Caruso, Bill Cayton, Milton Chwasky, Willie Cintron, Ann Coale, Al "Ice" Cole, Jim Coleman, Andrew Constantine II, Tom Cundy, Jeremy Dallow, John D'Angelo, Richard Davimos, Sr., Rich Davimos, Robert Davimos, Kery Davis, Morty Davis, Louis DeCubas, Joe DiMaggio, Joe DiVencenzo, Mike Donnelly, Dan Drykerman, Colleen Dunn, Dino Duva, Mark Eisner, Phil Eitman, Tom Emery, Pat English, Jeannie Evans, Lou Falcigno, Stu Feldman, David Finiger, Sheriff Armando Fontoura, Ron Fry (my publisher), Mark George, Frank Giantomasi, Joe Glodek, Sr., Joe Glodek, Jr., Eddie and Gilda Gold, Dan and Lisa Goldberg, Paul Goldstein, Steve Goldstein (Mr. Everything), Jeff Greenman, Kenny Greene, Roy Greenman, Ernie Grunfeld, Roger Haber, Steve Hamilton, Ron Heller, Drew Holder, Jerry Izenberg, Leonard Jaffe, Peter Janssen, Steve Kaplan, Ron Katz, Charles and Ann Kelman, Connor Killigan, Don King, Barry Klarberg, Herb Kozlov, Hersh Kozlov, Ron and Cheli Kramer, Brian Krauss, Cedric Kushner, Gabe LaConte, Jeff Lane, Diane Lavine, Bob Lee, Larry "Laurice" Lerman, Donna Lewan, Phil Lifschitz, Bruce Lipnick, Norman Logan, Peter Mangin, Melin Mansouri, Leon Margules, Vince Marold, Kevin Masarik, Charles Melone, Ray Mercer, Bruce Meyers, Scott and Lisa Miller, Andrea Motiero, Charles "The Natural" Murray, Danell Nicholson, Jim Nuckel, Tommy Parks, Tracy Patterson, Todd Roberti, Suzette Roberts, Peter Roselle, Gary Scharf, Art Sharples, Gene Silverman, staff at Angelo and Maxies (Howie Levine, Marc Miller, and Rich Wolf), Alan Stahler, State Bank of South Orange staff (Rose, Nancy, Sophia, Dave, and Diane), Emanuel Steward, Lyndon Stockton, David Strumeier, Howie Trinker, Alex Trujillo, Donald Trump, Sharon Velez, Kristina Vidov, Steve Wax, Alan Weingarten, Janine Weiss, Jeff Wilkes, Gary Weisman, Russell Weisman, Scott Waldman, Coach Gary Williams, Gary Wood, Jim Young.

Special thanks to my terrific staff at Worldwide Entertainment and Sports:

Joel Segal, Erik Rudolph, Mike Goodson, Ryan Schinman, Erica June, Carolos Albuerne, Claude Craft, Leonard Byam, Dave Caravantes, Vince Carroll, Mike Donnelly, Ron Dubiel, Tom Emery, Rene Farrow, Todd Goldenberg, Paul Goldstein, Roger Haber, Rahieme Ham, Sam Hampton, Matt Howard, my interns (Mark Consentino, Jamie Lomrantz, and Matt Friedman), Diane Lavine, Mike Mahone, Mike Mancuso, Leon Margules, James Mendez, Eddie Mustafa Muhammad, Todd Mury, Troy Parks, Tina Pecoriello, Percy Richardson, Jay Schulthess, Vicki Strowe, Troy Taylor, Barbara Wallace.

To all my teriffic cousins:

Steve Feit, Bonnie and Frank Duchon, Jeffrey Gold, Robert Gold, Jay and Renee Goret, David and Jill Goret, Howie and Ellen Jacobs, Irwin and Diane Jacobs, Jodi Jacobs, Nancy and Robert Lee, Jerry and Linda Schultz, David and Debbie Schultz, Shari and Harvey Schwartz, Danny and Lisa Subarsky, and Edy Subarsky.

To my publicists over the years:

Dan Klores, Shari Misher, Scott Moranda, Peter Seligman, Richard Valvo, and Bobby Zarem.

Special thanks to all the shareholders of Worldwide Entertainment and Sports. Thanks to all my investors who have shown such support throughout the years. There are too many of you to mention, but each of you is very special to me.

And finally, to all my clients, for being a proud part of Worldwide Entertainment and Sports (see client list on page 245).

Contents

Foreword

My old friend and colleague, the late Red Smith, once offered this classic definition of the Yiddish word "chutzpah," which scholars of the language generally translate as "brazen nerve":

"A fellow kills his mother and father and then throws himself on the mercy of the court because he's an orphan."

I figured that that was about as close as you could get to seeing chutzpah in action.

But then I met Marc Roberts.

Here is a guy who spent all of three semesters in college (one of them in summer school) and left, officially declaring his education completed, possibly because the professors in the only classes he bothered to visit (accounting and economics) asked him a lot of questions that he believed were none of their damn business...a fellow who, at age 19, sold the only asset he had—his car—and finished raising the $25,000 he needed to go into the boxing business—a business that, of course, he knew nothing about in the first place—by hanging around in the parking lot at a shopping mall in Livingston, N.J., and soliciting every person who got out of a Mercedes or Cadillac.

Squeegee men on New York street corners are less aggressive, which, if you understand chutzpah, should come as no surprise.

He raised money with chutzpah and made a profit off hard work.

Score: Roberts 1, Poverty 0—although he was living in an attic at the time.

After an experience like that, most guys living on the economic edge would proceed with caution, throwing their nickels around as if they were manhole covers. But off that kind of gamble was born a blend of chutzpah and determined tunnel vision that generated the business credo Roberts details in this book.

Roberts Rules!

Nowhere within its pages will you find the words "restraint," "introversion," or "safety first." If Marc Roberts's story were a Broadway musical, the big production number would be nine guys in baseball uniforms singing, "You gotta have chutzpah."

His ideas rate their own platform because of a simple, basic reason: They seem to work.

It is unclear whether his critics—and he has many in a business whose competition makes HBO's Arliss, the fictional sports agent, look like an Eagle Scout on Arbor Day—called him a fool because they couldn't figure out what he was doing or because there were times when he, himself, wasn't sure.

But he obviously figured it out.

Since those days in Livingston, he bought an interest in a Manhattan restaurant, became the first guy ever to take his stable of boxers public, absorbed several major sports agencies into a new organization, took that company public as well, and is becoming a force in that field from contract negotiations on down to endorsements for the clients his Worldwide Entertainment and Sports corporation represents.

Additionally, the kid who, with the aid of a janitor, set up 800 chairs in a high school gym so he could promote his first fight, is also on the verge of negotiating for his fighters purses whose numbers read like the area code for Saturn.

If you study the business strategy he lays down in his book, you have no choice but to conclude that beyond the frenetic work ethic, the relentless unabashed courtship of his clients, the staff-building and networking, remain two key ingredients that he values with equal, almost obsessive, passion. They are the principles that never made it into the Harvard Business School curriculum where they are viewed as blue-collar handicaps in a white-collar world: luck and chutzpah. The former, according to the late Branch Rickey, baseball's greatest innovator, is the residue of design. The latter is the catalyst for all the things you can do with that residue once you identify it.

Listen closely to what Marc says.

Remember, they don't teach chutzpah at the Wharton School.

—Jerry Izenberg

Introduction

You may be asking, "Who is Marc Roberts and why is he giving advice?"

This is a fair question, one that I think should be answered before you start reading my book. I am the president and chairman of Worldwide Entertainment and Sports (WWES on NASDAQ)—the first sports management company ever to be publicly traded on the stock market. Over the last 20 years (since I was 19 years old), I have become a major player in this fiercely competitive business and I have watched as the sports management industry has chewed up and spit out many very capable and ambitious people. So why have I been able to succeed here? Why have I been able to create a management company that has catapulted its way to the top? Why have I been described as a cross between P.T. Barnum and Donald Trump? So many people have asked these questions that I've decided to answer them in this book.

First, my background:

✓ I began promoting boxing shows in Plainfield, N.J., after dropping out of college at age 19.

✓ By age 20, I was arranging million-dollar endorsement deals for superstar boxer Thomas "Hitman" Hearns.

✓ Two years later, I was advisor to Donald Curry (former welterweight champion).

✓ In 1988, I formed the Triple Threat Enterprises boxing team by signing three exciting amateurs: 1988 Olympic heavyweight gold medalist Ray "Merciless" Mercer, junior welterweight Charles "The Natural" Murray, and light heavyweight Al "Ice" Cole.

✓ Since then, I have promoted more than 100 boxing events in places such as Madison Square Garden in New York City, casinos in Las Vegas, and the Convention Center in Atlantic City.

✓ In 1990, I became the first and only person to take a boxing management company (Triple Threat) public.

✓ In 1995, I became founder, president, and chairman of Worldwide Entertainment and Sports, representing not only big-name boxers, but also football and basketball players.

✓ In 1996, I was the first person to take a sports management company public. Worldwide Entertainment and Sports became available for public trading on NASDAQ.

✓ In the last two years, I have raised close to $12 million, with an initial public offering (IPO) of $8.4 million and a private placement of $3.5 million.

✓ My company has grown from about five athletes a year and a half ago to more than 60 today, including two of the top 10 rookies in the NBA, many superstars in the NFL, and two of the top five heavyweights in the world.

✓ I am a self-made multimillionaire.

That's who I am. That's what I've done. And because I've done all this at a very young age with nothing behind me but a relentless will to succeed and a belief in myself, I think I'm in a great position to offer some advice. I have a unique perspective to offer because no one has ever taken the path I've chosen to the top. I've tried it, it's worked, and now I'm ready to share with you what I've learned along the way.

What's the secret?

The business strategies and techniques I've used to reach my goals are called "secrets" in the book's title because I haven't revealed them before now. I don't have a business degree (or even a college degree). I've had a few wonderful mentors along the way, but all the theories I propose I've developed over the years through trial and error. I don't claim to be an Ivory-tower business consultant; I'm a self-made entrepreneur with real-world experiences to share. Although every step of my journey has been taken against the odds with nothing but street smarts and a relentless desire to win, I have come out on top. I've written this book to tell you how I did it—something I've never talked about publicly before. You are about to get an inside and up-close look at the secrets of my success.

Warning: This book will change your life

Before you begin, I should warn you: This is not a how-to program. There are no accompanying workbooks. There are no charts, no journals, no mapping of before-and-after accomplishments. There will be no seminars to explain how to implement the suggested strategies. I'm offering you simple, straightforward advice based on my own personal experiences. Anyone from a high school dropout to a Harvard Ph.D. can pick up this book and use it as a blueprint for success—right now, today. If you start reading this minute, one-half hour from now you'll already have a new tool or two that will enable you to become immediately more productive and gain an advantage over others in your field.

I honestly have no doubt that this book will change your life. It will teach you how to overcome odds, to face adversity, and to get motivated. It will teach you how to network, to focus, to stand out, to get attention, to deal with your enemies, to tune into your own inner voice, to build a reputation, and so on. And you'll learn these things, not from any lectures, but through example. As you read about my business dealings, you'll find yourself asking questions: "If Roberts can negotiate multimillion-dollar deals without a penny in his pocket, why shouldn't I?" "If he can listen to his gut and turn down the advice of his family, friends, and colleagues, why shouldn't I?" "If he can stage big press events to get his company's name in the news, why shouldn't I?" "If he can build a strong network of supporters and backers and have a load of fun at the same time, why can't I?"

That's the point: I've already done all these things and more, and they've given me wealth and success beyond my dreams. Why shouldn't you use the same strategies and enjoy the same benefits?

Daily inspiration

I have filled this book with quotable quotes that will encourage you each day to navigate through the minefield of your own career. Look for tips like this one:

When people tell you you're crazy, that's a good sign that you're on the right track. When your competitors tell you you're no good and you're a failure, that means you're on to something big.

You need to get up every morning ready to go and open to all the possibilities the day may bring. These little pieces of advice are motivational tools you can carry around in your head and repeat to yourself over and over when you are in danger of straying from the path that will lead you to your goal.

My guarantee

To get all the details of successful entrepreneuring, all you have to do is start reading. Open the book to Rule #1 and give it a fair shot. If you add the suggested business practices to your own experiences and couple them with unwavering determination, I guarantee you'll find success in whatever you do. In fact, if you follow the principles mapped out in each chapter and then can honestly say that you haven't learned anything that can change your life, you can have your money back. That's how sure I am that this book has the power to change lives.

You can contact me at:

Worldwide Entertainment and Sports
29 Northfield Ave., Suite 200
West Orange, NJ 07052
e-mail: info@wwentertainment.com

—Marc Roberts
June 1998

Go for It!

I don't take a "walk-before-you-run" approach to anything. It's my experience that success belongs to aggressive people—the ones who are willing to take risks and go for it. Before you make any plans for your future, check your personal supply of persistence, determination, and ambition. They're better indicators of success than anything else you have.

Right out of high school, I decided to go for it by jumping into a place where everyone said I didn't belong. I wanted to play Division One basketball at American University in Washington, D.C. Everyone thought I should sign with any one of the many Division II schools recruiting me and consider myself lucky. "After all," they reminded me, "you're a talented shooter—but you're also a short, white kid."

But that's not what I wanted. So I made a deal with the coach from American University: If I went out for the team and made it, he'd get me a scholarship. Feeling pretty proud of my brilliant plan, I headed off to American U.

Right after I registered for classes, that coach left the school without telling anybody about our deal. Now I had to wrangle the same agreement with the new coach. If I remember correctly, "fat chance" was the only encouragement I heard from my family and friends. The other guys at the tryout were *big*: seven feet, six-10, six-six, and all African-American. It didn't look good for the scrawny little white kid.

Once you announce you're going for it, friends and colleagues will have a lot to say: "You can't do that." "You'll get eaten up alive." "You're in way over your head." I've learned to use these discouraging words as a source of motivation. When people try to knock you down, you've got to work harder to prove them wrong.

The big decision

I proved them all wrong—sort of. I made the team, but I didn't get my scholarship. But as it turned out, that was okay because when I was on the team, I made a friend who would eventually turn my life around. Russell "Boo" Bowers, the leading scorer in the country, was on the American U team. There wasn't a basketball fan who didn't know Bowers's name. He was fantastic, but he had a problem: Sports agents from around the country were all over him—at the gym, at his dorm, at lunch, after his classes. He couldn't move a muscle without having an agent in his face. Finally, the heavy recruiting started to affect his concentration and his game and the coach went nuts. He ordered all agents off the campus. Word got out fast that no one was allowed to recruit Bowers during the season. This situation was a once-in-a-lifetime opportunity for me.

If you're going to be successful, you have to know what opportunity looks like when it's staring you in the face.

I practiced with this guy every day; we traveled together all over the country; I lived in the dorm room next to his. Who knew Boo Bowers better than I did? And who now had exclusive access to him? I decided I wanted to be his agent. Why not? The fact that I knew nothing at all about managing an athlete didn't make me crazy (as many claimed); it made me determined to find out more.

I knew being an agent had something to do with signing contracts, so I called a friend who was a lawyer. I knew Roy Greenman, who had been my camp counselor years before, wouldn't laugh at the idea. Roy introduced me to his friend and partner, Arnie Budin; they helped me form a company, and at the age of 19, I signed Bowers as my first client.

Jumping into a situation where I had no experience may seem risky, but this approach to life is the foundation of my success. The first rule of this book is *Go for It!* because it is the first rule I live by. The opportunity was there; it wasn't going to come again. I had to grab on and go for the ride.

What you lack in experience, make up for with an overload of motivation, dedication, and ambition.

A risky step

Now I had dollar signs in my eyes. I wanted to be a great sports agent and become disgustingly wealthy. In my sophomore year of college, I had an economics professor who claimed he knew the process and method of becoming a millionaire—he had my full attention. I listened hard; I really wanted to learn, but something about his plan just didn't seem right. How did he know if these strategies and methods really worked? Had he tried them out? Did real life actually work like the textbooks describe?

I decided to follow this professor after class one day to learn more about him. I found out that this highly credentialed, academically astute guy who claimed to know the secrets of wealth and fortune was driving a 12-year-old rusty heap without hubcaps or a muffler. Something seemed to have gone wrong in his formula for wealth. I followed him as he drove off spitting and spurting black exhaust fumes. He pulled up to a decrepit apartment house in a rundown neighborhood. This guy was going to teach me how to become a millionaire? I don't think so.

Before you accept any information as fact, evaluate the source. Ask yourself: Has this person been there? What has he or she accomplished?

I decided I couldn't take another two-and-a-half years of getting second-hand information that couldn't be applied in the real world. This time, going for it meant leaving school. I wanted to be an entrepreneur, a self-employed businessman, a participant in the American Dream. I thought these were admirable goals. My parents disagreed. They were furious that I would give up my education, my future. At best, they hoped I was just going through a phase that would pass. So to keep the peace, I agreed to a compromise: I would take a leave of absence rather than quit outright. They were sure I'd be back; I was positive I wouldn't.

My parents figured the deck was stacked in their favor. With a little real-world shock therapy, they were sure I'd be back the next semester. They threw me out of the house; they took back the car. They stopped all funding and allowances. They sat back and waited for me to come home begging to return to school. But for somebody like me, this was a challenge, not a setback. I was even more determined to stay out of school and be successful. Having to sacrifice personal comforts made me feel more of an urgency to make it to the top faster. If they hadn't "starved" me, what would be the hurry?

When you go for it, you'll probably have to sacrifice something you have now: maybe security, maybe income, maybe status. This fact will push you in one of two ways: 1) You'll either be so nervous about this loss that you won't be able to get anything done, or 2) You'll be so determined to make up for the loss that nothing will stop you. There's no place in the middle. You have to pick a side.

I moved into an attic in Summit, N.J., with a roommate. It sounded impressive to say that I was a sports agent, but at that point my "profession" wasn't paying the bills. So my first move was to get a job that could support my career. I started commuting into New York to work on Wall Street on the commodities floor. Even though this wasn't what I wanted to do forever, this was a great job for two reasons: First, this is the place to meet a lot of big investors who don't know what to do with all of their money (I knew I'd need this information down the line). Second, work was over at 2:30 p.m. every day—this gave me time to build up my real business as a sports agent.

Jumping into business—ready or not

I signed a few more basketball players; I signed a baseball umpire. Then the local paper wrote an article about my agency. This little article opened up another door that people warned me to stay away from—so of course I just had to run through it.

I got a call from a guy named Sarge Esposito who saw the article. "How'd you like to manage some fighters?" he asked. It flashed through my mind that I didn't know one thing about fighters, but I did know I would be willing to manage a snail at that point. "Sounds good!" I said. "How can we get started?"

We met at a gym in Plainfield, N.J., where there were a bunch of muscle-bound guys about my age working out. "Which ones are the toughest kids in here?" I asked. Esposito pointed out three strong and fast fighters. "I'll take all three," I said. Why pick one, I figured, if all three were available?

I soon learned why I should have taken only one. The trainer sat me down and mapped out all the stuff he and his fighters needed. "We need salaries we can live on, we need food money, training money, and spending money so the fighters can concentrate on training and winning." I didn't have a clue what I was doing, but I figured if I had about 25 grand, I could make it work.

I went back to the lawyers and they assured me that they didn't have $25,000, but they said I could start a limited partnership to raise the money. I didn't know what the hell they were talking about, but I always believed that when something sounds too complicated, all I have to do is break it down into its simplest form so I can work with it. What they were trying to tell me was that I could get *all* the money by asking lots of people for *some* of the money. What I really needed was only $2,500—from 10 different people. This was doable. Over the next few months, I begged hundreds of people for the money, and soon I had the 10 people I needed.

I signed my first three fighters and set out to get them fights. I quickly learned that this is not easy to do when you don't know anybody in the business. I called all over the country looking for someone to fight these guys. I couldn't get them a fight in a back ally behind a bar, nothing.

Then finally, I got a fight for my number-one guy with a fight promoter named Vito Tolerito in Hartford, Conn. With my buddies along for support, we all drove up there for this pro debut in a packed house with a bunch of good fights. My guy got in the ring against a local Hartford fighter and right off the bat my fighter was beating the heck out of this other guy. Beating him from post to post, killing him. At the end of the four-round fight, we were cheering and celebrating and congratulating all over the place. Then came the official decision—my fighter lost the fight!

I had my first big common-sense learning experience in boxing: It is always preferential to seek a neutral location for a fight. Okay, so now that I had this little piece of insider info, how could I use it to work for me instead of against me? The answer was obvious: Before I even got back home that night, I had decided to promote a fight in my fighter's hometown in Plainfield, N.J.

I wanted to fight all three of my guys in a big, blow-out boxing event. But nobody had promoted a fight in Plainfield or anywhere near that area in more than 20 years; all the fights were going to Atlantic City back then. And the boxing commissioner said I needed a license to promote a fight. No problem. I figured I'd get a license. I called Bob Lee, who is now the head of the International Boxing Federation, but who was then the state athletic commissioner. I told him my name, and he asked how old I was. I told him and he laughed. He asked if I had ever been involved with boxing, and I said no. He asked if I had ever laced on a pair of gloves before, and I said no. He asked if I knew anything about boxing, and I said no. He asked if I had a friend or anybody who could teach me, and I said, "No, Mr. Lee, not really at all." He drew in a deep breath and then barked at me: "Are you crazy? I'm going to give you the best advice you're ever gonna get. After you hang up this phone, turn away from boxing and run as fast as you can away from this sport. Believe me, you'll lose your shirt. This is a cut-throat business that will chew up and spit out a guy like you." I said, "Well, thanks for the advice," and I hung up. This obviously was just one more time that I would have to ignore a "knowledgeable" person and go for it anyway.

When people tell you you're crazy, it's a good sign that you're on the right track. When your competitors tell you you're no good and you're a failure, that means you're on to something big.

Learning the ropes

I found someone who did have a license, I made him my co-promoter, and legally promoted my fight. Now my real education began. I was about to venture into an area of sports promoting that no classroom course could have prepared me for, no book could have explained, and where no timid person should ever venture.

For the next three months, I did everything. First, I sold my car to get the $10,000 I guessed it would take to put on a fight. Then, I quit my job because it was taking up too much of my time. (I got a good job selling computer supplies on my own clock.) I spent every spare minute working to put this fight together (many times until three and four in the morning). I did everything from ordering the tickets and making posters, to arranging hotel rooms for the fighters, filing contracts, and setting up chairs. I did *everything*.

Once you decide to go for it, you've got to stay focused. You've got to eat, breathe, and sleep whatever it is you're doing.

There's no doubt that I learned a lot about sports promoting from this experience. But I also learned that sometimes no matter how hard you work, it's dumb luck that really makes the difference. The day before the fight, I had almost zero tickets sold. I was dying because I had invested so much time and money. You can bet I started to doubt the wisdom of jumping in blind and following the go-for-it philosophy. But then the day of the fight, people just kept coming and coming and coming—the place was sold out! People were practically climbing in through the air vents. I was a genius! Well, actually, I was lucky. That was the day I learned an important lesson about staging an event: Know your crowd, know what's going on in their lives on the date of your event. In this case, I just happened to pick the day for the fight when the residents of this inner city got their welfare checks— the day when they had money in hand to spend. Without knowing it, I had used a brilliant piece of marketing strategy.

Although I think it was a miracle that the whole thing came off at all, it turned out to be a great night. The crowd had a wild time—they loved it. I had invited a bunch of heavy-hitting investors who I hoped would help me in the future. It was a good time, really perfect— especially because all of my guys won. To this day I don't know how it happened. I was working with nothing more than common sense and a willingness to go for what I wanted with a whole lot of enthusiasm and energy.

If you decide to go for it, at some point there will be risk involved—eventually, you'll find yourself flying without a net. But that's what makes it so exciting and worthwhile. If you want to be an entrepreneur in any profession, you have to be able to live with risk, because you can't get ahead of everybody else without sticking your neck out.

Graduation

Over the next year, I put together two more fights just like that one. Each one was better than the last. These fights were my graduation into sports management. I had taken the course in the school of hard knocks, paid some dues, and was ready to launch my career. I learned more in those three fights than I could ever have learned in four years of college. I still wasn't making any money, but I was in heaven. And most important, I had proven that I wasn't a loser because I had dropped out of college.

This experience also taught me a very valuable lesson: When you have the guts to take a giant step toward something you really want, the people around you aren't going to cheer you on. You're doing something that they're scared to do, and whether it's out of good intentions or out of jealousy, they're going to root against you. Maybe it's human nature. Whatever the reason for the put-downs, you have to get past them. If you want to go for something very important in your life, accept criticism as normal and keep moving forward—never look back.

Critical life lessons

- ✓ Don't always walk before you run.
- ✓ Use discouraging comments such as, "You'll get eaten alive," to fuel your determination.
- ✓ Be open to opportunity.
- ✓ Don't let a lack of experience slow you down. Make up for it with excess motivation, determination, persistence, and ambition.
- ✓ Don't be afraid of sacrifice; it's a great motivator.

✓ Be critical of "experts" who tell you how its done, unless they've already done it.

✓ When people tell you you're crazy, it's a good sign that you're on the right track.

✓ Eat, breathe, and sleep your goals.

✓ Risk is good; you can't get ahead of everybody else unless you're willing to stick your neck out.

✓ Go for it and don't look back.

Sell With Pizzazz

Maybe your resume doesn't list "salesperson" as your occupation, but if you want to be successful in business—any business—you need to learn how to sell your product or service better than anyone else on the block. Sales isn't a job only for salespeople; it's the occupation of everyone who wants to make it big.

Over the next eight years, my company, Marc Roberts Boxing, Inc., promoted my three boxers: Ray "Merciless" Mercer, the 1988 heavyweight Olympic gold medal champion; Charles "The Natural" Murray, a junior welterweight; and Al "Ice" Cole, a cruiserweight. They achieved a combined record of 49 wins and zero losses. This record sounds impressive, but it wasn't quite enough to fight for the big purses. So even with their combined wins, my business was operating in the red. My expenses were outrageous. I had two trainers, two bookkeepers, a full-time strength coach, and a couple of gofers on my payroll. I also had to pay salaries to the boxers, plus I gave them a total of $150,000 in bonuses over a three-year period.

Before too long, I and my investors had put more than $1 million into the business, and I figured it would take another million to keep it going. I didn't want to liquidate any more of my personal assets, so I thought, "Why not go to Wall Street and take my business public?" At the time that I got this big idea, I didn't even know what a stock was. I just knew in my own naive way that if you took your company public, you were sharing your company and you got a lot of money. That idea sounded good, but even I knew my company (now called Triple Threat Enterprises because when I decided to go public, I wanted investors to focus on the fighters, not on my name) would be a tough sell.

Triple Threat Enterprises operated in the red since day one. This meant that every dollar invested would be purely on speculation, because there was no guarantee that the company would ever make money. But still, I wanted to do an underwriting for $3.5 million.

Even if Triple Threat had been a financial success, the sale of a boxing management company wouldn't be easy. I was trying to sell something that no one had ever tried selling before. Nobody ever puts money into a boxer until he starts making money because boxing is such a risky business. It's so difficult to figure out who is going to go all the way to the top and be the world's champion.

To top it all off, I decided to do this in November 1991. Needless to say, the Persian Gulf War was still making the stock market shaky. Nobody on Wall Street was doing initial public offerings (IPOs) on anything!

The winners of the world are not afraid to step out of the crowd and be different. They recognize the challenge ahead and are prepared to hurdle all obstacles in their way.

Packaging a sale

With all this against me, I knew I had to do something that would make my company look irresistible. I had to "package" my product to make it sizzle. I learned fast that all successful businesspeople are also excellent salespeople. I couldn't just sit in my gym thinking that if I were a really good sports agent, the rest would fall into place, that people would find out about me and start throwing money my way. It just doesn't happen. To be successful, you have to know how to sell yourself and your product and service to make it stand out from the crowd and make it irresistible to investors or customers.

To impress potential investors, I hired someone to produce a highlight video featuring my three fighters. Naturally, the video showed only shots of them knocking out other fighters. I also showed them being interviewed, and again, the tape featured only the best interviews. Then I had some boxing experts face the camera and give their "expert" opinions on how amazing my three fighters were. "It will be very unlucky," one of the experts said, "if Mercer, Murray, and Cole don't make millions of dollars."

This is how you sell. Brag, boast, highlight. Use technology, action, color, experts. Sell a feeling. Sell potential. Sell!

I also put a lot of time into preparing a mailing list that would show investors I had a network of contacts already in place. I organized the list I had been creating of more than 8,000 people who had attended my fights. I knew once I got it structured properly, and if I put in the time and effort to call every person on the list, I could find some investors right there.

Selling is a numbers game—the more calls you make, the more sales you'll have. Highly successful salespeople get what they're after through sheer persistence.

Selling excitement

All of this was a good start, but it wasn't enough to raise the kind of money I wanted. I had to do something more, something big to attract big money. I decided I needed something that would show how serious I was about this venture. I wanted potential investors to know I wasn't going to get bored or discouraged and move on to something else if the fighters started losing. I wanted to have something that would emphasize my work ethic and my attitude. I knew that if I could convince people I was sincere and ethical, I'd have a better shot at getting their money. I needed something large and concrete.

I decided to build a spectacular boxing facility in Newark, N.J. I poured half a million dollars into a 13,000-square-foot warehouse and equipped it with a beautiful boxing gym with saunas and whirlpools, two boxing rings, and a state-of-the-art weight room. It was gorgeous. People said I was crazy to put so much money into just a gym, but that was exactly my plan. It was outrageous. It was unique. It was a sure-fire way to get a lot of publicity and attract investors. I knew somehow I'd make economic sense out of it.

The right product will get you in anyone's door. But to consummate the sale, you'd better have a great package. Selling almost always involves an element of showmanship to dramatize the message, to create excitement, and to hold the attention of the client.

After I put this "sales package" together, I set out to find someone on Wall Street who would feel excited about my concept. That person turned out to be Jack Dell, who was a consultant on Wall Street. I invited Dell to visit my boxing facility. I could tell he was in awe. The gym looked spectacular; my fighters were doing great (Ray Mercer was undefeated; Charles Murray was being called the next Sugar Ray Leonard; and Al Cole was destined to become a champion). And by the time Dell finished watching my video, he was hooked. His interest was in show business, and that's exactly what I was selling. It was glitz galore!

People with money are always looking for an outlet for that money. But it's not just a question of who has the money to invest, but more important, who has a passion for your idea. That's true of securing money for any project.

Dell's firm wanted a big piece of the investment for itself, so it was not permitted to underwrite the IPO. But through the firm's contacts, we hooked up with D.H. Blair Investment Banking Corp., a major brokerage house that also had strong distribution capabilities. And the process of going public began.

In the middle of selling my company to investors, I hit a good-luck break. Ray Mercer fought for the WBO Heavyweight Championship against Francisco Damiani. Mercer lost every round for the first eight rounds; in the ninth round he hit Damiani with an incredible shot to the nose that split it wide open. Damiani went face down on the canvas and was out for about 10 minutes. If Mercer hadn't won that fight, I don't know if I ever would have gone public.

But he did win, and I did go public. All in all, the sale generated $3.5 million. I raised about half the money off my mailing list, and the brokers raised the other half. I received $1 million in cash (alleviating me of about $1 million worth of liability), plus a million shares in the company. The arrangement also enabled me to draw a large salary and even a big bonus. Later, I sold my remaining shares, netting close to $4 million. I was barely 30 years old.

Whether you're selling an idea or a specific product, or raising money for your company or trying to get people to attend a charity event, you need to develop a positive attitude and a razzle-dazzle approach that puts you out in front of the pack.

Selling a dream

What made the whole thing so interesting was what I was selling. I was selling a dream! Jack Dell wanted to be in the entertainment field. Although some people don't realize it, professional sports is as much a part of show business today as is the Broadway theater or the movie industry. And the individual investors who invested $1,000 or $2,000 in Triple Threat stock were also buying a dream. They wanted to have a small piece of a fighter. Most people, if they wanted to invest in a fighter, would have to spend a lot of money. Here, by owning Triple Threat stock, every time Mercer, Murray, or Cole got into the ring, each investor could say, "Hey, see that guy? He's my fighter."

You have to identify exactly what you're selling. I couldn't sell a then-unprofitable boxing company in the middle of a shaky stock market—but I could sell a dream based on the prospects of future earnings, especially with the fighters I had, including gold-medal winner Ray Mercer. I could sell something exciting and intangible. I could sell a chance to grab on to a piece of stardom. I found a way to get people excited about something fun and unique. That's the key. You have to look beyond the mundane facts of your product or service and find something that people can get excited about, something they are willing to take a risk for. Everyone has the power and talent to promote and sell something that is unique. The tough part is getting in touch with that unique selling point.

Too many would-be businesspeople assume that selling is just knowing about the product or service and going out and telling others. Or they believe that building a better mousetrap guarantees that the world will beat a path to their door. They're wrong.

If you're in your own business, selling is going to be a constant in your life. For example, borrowing money from a bank to run a business is not simply a matter of submitting numbers and sitting back and waiting for someone else to make a decision. It involves selling your idea and yourself to a banker who is a very special kind of "client." Smart entrepreneurs go to great lengths to get to know their bankers and stay on good terms with them. And the same thing applies when you create a business plan and go out to raise money for your company or idea: You're largely engaged in a process of selling.

Recruiting others to join you in a business venture is also selling. Let's say you want to hire Joe—you need his financial skills. But you're worried about asking Joe to join your team because Joe has a job, and a wife, and two kids, and a dog, and a mortgage. You're squeamish about persuading Joe to quit the job he has now because you worry, "What if things don't work out?"

Come on! Will Joe join your venture if *you* are afraid you're going to fail? No way! Half-hearted missionaries don't make converts. You need to sell Joe, and everyone else, on your dream. In the early part of your enterprise, that dream may be all the assets you have—make it look like the buy of the century.

Critical life lessons

✓ Sales isn't a job only for salespeople; it's the occupation of everyone who wants to make it big.

✓ Whatever your product is, package it so that it sizzles.

✓ Many highly successful salespeople get what they're after through sheer persistence.

✓ Selling almost always involves an element of showmanship to dramatize the message.

✓ Sell what's good, unique, and special. Ignore the rest.

✓ Sell with excitement, confidence, and unwavering enthusiasm.

Put a Spin on Trouble

I believe 100 percent that the only way to learn about success is through trial and error. This means you'll get your butt kicked a few times, but in every moment of adversity, there is a lesson that will help you in the future.

I don't go looking for trouble, and I'm not too anxious to take on the challenge of setbacks. But the fact is, if you've got lots of ambition and you're going to stick your neck out, occasionally you're going to have to deal with adversity. I know I wouldn't be in the position I'm in today if I hadn't been kicked around a bit. And there's no doubt I'll be facing more obstacles in the future—it's part of taking risks and being in charge. But every setback has taught me something that has helped me get even further ahead. Three steps forward, one step back is often the footwork of successful people.

The first hostile takeover in boxing

Going public with Triple Threat Enterprises was the best decision I ever made, but even good decisions can turn against you. In November 1991, about a year after we went public, my fighter Ray Mercer fought Tommy Morrison for the Heavyweight Championship of the World. It was a great fight. Mercer was losing in the beginning, but then in the fifth round, Mercer knocked Morrison out cold. This was one of the most brutal knockouts in boxing history. Morrison eventually got up and returned to his stool where he sat throwing punches in an imaginary fight that was still going on in his head. He was out of it. I was ecstatic—this was my dream come true. The fighter who I had worked with from the moment he won his gold medal in the Seoul Olympics was now a multimultimillion-dollar fighter. I partied all night long and went to bed about 5 a.m. feeling on top of the world.

A few hours later, Jack Dell called me. (Jack, if you remember, was the financial consultant for my initial public offering.) He said he needed to see me right away. So I rushed over, still grinning from ear to ear. Without any warning, Jack ripped my heart out. "Listen," he said, "I brought you up here to tell you that, as of this moment, I'm the new manager of Ray Mercer and Triple Threat Enterprises. Thanks for all your hard work; you did a great job." I thought I couldn't have heard right. Was he saying that from now on he was going to be taking credit for all the things I had worked so hard for?

It turned out that Jack had been buying up Triple Threat stock right out from under me and had developed a cozy relationship with Mercer's trainer which may have convinced Mercer that he should sign with Dell. I couldn't believe what I was hearing. How could I lose everything I had put together?

After about two weeks of legal meetings and positioning, I had two options: 1) I could fight the takeover. This could cost millions, which I didn't have. Even if I won, I'd be subject to a shareholders' lawsuit for interfering with the operation of Triple Threat. Or 2) I could take the offered million-dollar buyout and leave the company. Either way, I'd lose something very important to me. I took option number two and became the world's saddest 30-year-old millionaire.

I couldn't believe what had happened to me—I was in shock for the next two months. I couldn't bear to even open a newspaper or turn on the TV. The headlines said I was fired (this was untrue but still humiliating), and because Mercer was so big after that fight, he was everywhere. Every radio station, TV channel, magazine, and newspaper reminded me of what had happened. There was no escaping or forgetting.

I knew that being a sports agent wasn't going to be an easy career—but I can't say I ever expected to get my insides torn out by the people closest to me.

Anyway, one day led to another until eventually I got my drive and enthusiasm back. I figured there had to be a way to put a positive spin on this; I was just going to have to dig really deep to find it.

For one thing, I decided to change the way I looked at being stabbed in the back. Actually, the experience had been an historic first: It was the first time a boxer had lost his manager due to a hostile takeover. Hey, again I'm breaking new ground!

And two, I figured I had learned an important business lesson that would help me in the future: I would never again take my finger off the pulse of the financial end of my work.

And three, I had to figure that something this catastrophic couldn't happen two times in a row. I was due for a streak of some great luck.

It was time to stop licking my wounds and get out there and try again. What else can you do? When you get the crap kicked out of you, you can't stay down. That's the biggest loss of all. You let your opponents win and you never get even. You've got to look into that place where your original determination and enthusiasm sprang from and dip into that well again.

When you get knocked down, no one can say you're finished if you keep getting back up.

The torn ligament disaster

Losing Triple Threat Enterprises wasn't the first time I had lost something for which I had worked hard and taken big risks. My very first step in managing athletes turned out to be a step into quicksand. As I mentioned earlier, my basketball teammate Boo Bowers was my meal ticket out of college. I figured when he told his teammates how well I was handling his career, I'd sign everybody. I knew he was key to making my sports agency fly.

Then the whole thing fell apart. In one of his last college games, Bowers dove after a loose ball and tore the ligaments in his knee. That was it. Twenty years ago they didn't have the surgical techniques they have today. Bowers never really recovered, and he never played in the NBA. Obviously, this was devastating for Bowers; it was not good for me either.

This was a time to make a big decision. I had left school banking on this one player. What should I do now? It wasn't too late to go back to school—maybe my parents would even start talking to me again. But if I went back to school, nothing would be different. I'd still be *reading* about things I wanted to be *doing*. So I figured I'd look for the bright side of things and focus all my attention there.

The bright side of this disaster was the fact that I now had the experience of signing a top recruit. This was my entree into the business; I was in. I was alone and penniless, but I was in and I wasn't going to give up now. I think if this kind of thing were to happen to me today, maybe I'd be more devastated than I was at the time. But back then, my level of determination was so high, I just couldn't consider defeat. I had to find the positive and run with it.

There's a positive side to everything—it's up to you to find it and use it to your advantage.

The rock and roll money pit

I was about 24 when I heard about a talented rock group that needed a manager. I thought it might be a good idea to diversify, so I listened to the band and thought they sounded pretty good (keeping in mind that I knew nothing about music and what made it good or bad). I took their tape to a lot of people in the music business and asked their opinion; everybody loved this group. Even people at CBS Records were enthusiastic about the band's sound. I figured I was onto something great.

I wanted to work closely with these guys and make sure they were managed properly, so I moved the two lead singers right into my house and started dishing out the money. I paid for new instruments, for practice sessions, studio time, and demo tapes. When they moved out, I paid the rent on their own apartment. I shopped their tape all over New York. I gave them my best effort (and my money) but I found out that it wasn't enough.

In my enthusiasm to promote their sound, I had overlooked the people themselves. It turned out that one of the singers couldn't perform live; he would choke up and couldn't sing. I had seen this in basketball when a player is great at practice but can't find the backboard in the game. Well, I was learning that the same thing can happen to a vocalist. The other singer was lazy. He'd miss practice sessions; he'd always want to leave early. He just didn't have the fire you need to make it big.

When I finally saw the problems, I decided it was time to stop putting my money into their future. Once the money stopped, the group immediately split up. These musicians obviously didn't have the determination and ambition that anyone who wants to be successful in a competitive field has to have.

I was young and the money I lost meant a lot to me, but I was learning. I bet on the wrong horse because I was convinced that my own enthusiasm could make any horse a winner. I didn't realize at that time that 80 percent of the formula for success is finding the right horse. Now I know that even if I do my job perfectly, even if my own levels of determination and ambition are at the highest point, the people I manage have to have the talent and the will to do their job at a top level of performance, too.

What price tag would you put on this information? This year, one semester of MBA study at Harvard costs $12,500. People pay this kind of money all the time and consider it a sound investment in knowledge. Why should the money I spend to learn the important lessons that fuel my success be viewed any differently? Life is a very large classroom. Sometimes the lessons are expensive, but those are the ones from which you usually learn the most.

Before you invest money in someone's business, or take on a partner, or financially back anything, make sure the people involved want success just as much as you do.

The NFL deal that got away

John Flood, who used to be the president of NFL Properties (the large NFL organization that licenses NFL products), was an old family friend. When we were about 19 years old, we decided to recruit football players together. In our first joint venture, we went after Howie Long out of Villanova. John had had some phone conversations with him and Howie seemed very open to our offer. So I went out to Villanova to clinch the deal.

I hung out at the college all weekend looking for chances to talk to Howie about all the things John and I could do for him. We talked endorsements, appearances, contracts, salaries, everything. By the time the weekend was over, Howie was very excited about signing with us. I called John and told him to get the contract ready—Howie Long was as good as signed. I left the campus feeling great.

After that day, I couldn't even get a phone call through to Howie. As soon as I left, other agents came in and swept him away; they had him sign immediately while he was still nodding his head yes. Wow, did I learn fast. You can't count on a verbal commitment. You can't take any agreement for granted until the deal is done—signed. No matter what they tell you, stay close by and see it through to the end. Losing Howie Long was a major loss. He turned out to be an all-pro player for about 12 years (who'll probably end up in the Hall of Fame), and is now one of the top sports analysts on TV and an actor in movies such as *Firestorm*.

Stay on top of your game. There's always somebody who is hungrier and more ambitious than you waiting in the wings to steal away what you think is in the bag.

Bad things happen when you're not looking

John "Up-the-Ladder" Williamson was a great basketball player for the New Jersey Nets during the days of Julius Erving. I recruited Williamson when I was really young and was shocked when he signed with me. This was another move that I thought would really propel me into sports management. I knew that with a big name on my roster, it would be easier to get others to sign on. So with this piece of success in my pocket, I ran off to recruit more big-name athletes. I spent that summer running after everybody who would listen to me. I had no idea that I was losing ground every hour I was away. While I was gone, Williamson ate himself out of a job—he blew up 50 pounds! He didn't even make the team when the season rolled around.

Sometimes adversity just hits out of the blue without any obvious cause. Sometimes you bring it on yourself. This time, I caused the problem. As his advisor, it was my responsibility to look after Williamson and keep him in shape. I had neglected him, and we both paid the price. I had lost sight of what was most important. I had forgotten my original plan to be the best manager in the business—not the best recruiter. I felt bad for me, but I felt awful for Williamson.

That was the last time I didn't make sure that a player stayed in top-flight shape after I recruited him.

Just because you have signed a contract doesn't mean you're finished. You have to service your clients and respect their needs.

The boxing decision rip-off

In 1996, I was managing Ray Mercer again. (That story—how I got my fighters back after the buyout of Triple Threat Enterprises—is a story for another time.) Mercer fought Lennox Lewis in an important match and lost a 10-round decision. "Robbery" is the only word that comes to mind when I think of that night. Even the press called the fight a "rip-off." Only in the sport of boxing could a fighter beat the heck out of someone from London in Madison Square Garden with the whole crowd chanting, "U.S.A.! U.S.A.!" and then lose the fight. So what could I do? How should I deal with things that are so unjust?

I quickly learned that there's nothing you can do. Plain and simple: Life's not fair. Sometimes things turn in your favor and sometimes they turn against you. It's not personal and you don't always have to feel like you have to do something about all of life's inequities. I have to believe that in the course of a career, things balance themselves out. All I can do is keep working hard, move on, and wait patiently for the decision to go my way.

Climbing back to the top

Hoping to balance the failures and successes of my career thus far, I decided to create a new public company called Worldwide Entertainment and Sports (WWES). I now had an expanded stable of boxers, including heavyweight superstar Shannon Briggs, as well as Ray Mercer, Al Cole, and Charles Murray

At the time I was in the middle of getting a commitment from an investment banker to raise money for a new public company, I had a big Friday-night fight in Atlantic City set up to put the spotlight on Briggs. HBO even did a five-minute feature on him before the fight. This was going to be the night that would sell Worldwide Entertainment and Sports. The house was packed with stockbrokers, investors,

---

and Briggs fans. The place was full of people who were interested in WWES going public.

Briggs threw a flurry of punches that stunned Darroll Wilson in the first minute of the first round. The crowd was looking for a quick knockout. By the end of the first round, Wilson recovered and connected with some punches of his own. As the third round began, the crowd sat back, thinking the fight would last longer than anticipated. But then something went very wrong. We know now that it was an asthma attack that let a club fighter take down Shannon Briggs—out cold. Briggs laid motionless and the referee immediately stopped the fight.

People have told me that angry bettors stormed out of the arena, having lost too much money to stick around for the official announcement. Other fans stood motionless waiting for the ring announcer to say what they couldn't believe: a Wilson knockout. I don't know what happened—I was already out of there.

I went into total shock. I started pinching myself because I couldn't believe this wasn't just a bad dream. I spent that whole weekend jumping back and forth between shock and denial. My apartment looked like a funeral home with friends dropping by in a steady stream to offer their condolences on the death of Worldwide Entertainment and Sports.

Monday morning it was time for damage control. Originally, I was selling Worldwide to investors based on the future of Shannon Briggs. Now I had to think of a way to put a positive twist on what had happened. This was a true test of salesmanship.

There are advantages and disadvantages to every situation. Make sure that you always harp on the advantages—always. Find your strengths and use them.

Work from a position of strength

Working from a position of strength was not a new idea for me. I had been highlighting the good and downplaying the bad ever since I got into this business. How do you think I got big-name athletes to sign with *me*—a no-name? Well, I may never have been a sports agent before, but that didn't mean I had nothing to bring to the venture. From the very beginning, I had to look at myself and the situation and find a way to compensate for my lack of experience. I knew that I could make athletes like me and want to sign with me; I just had to find a way to make myself look like the best agent around. Most people felt my young age was a strike against me, so that's where I decided to focus my efforts; I just turned this "problem" around to my advantage.

I told the athletes that they should sign with me because I was young and enthusiastic. I convinced these athletes that the older agents didn't have the energy or the time that I had and that because I was younger, I understood what they needed. My young age became my key selling point. (Of course, now that I'm older, my strength is the exact opposite: I sell my experience and my track record.)

Thinking back on this strategy that had worked for me in the past, I decided to use it again to convince my investors to stay with me. I knew that if I was going to make this work, I couldn't go into the brokerage house half-heartedly with self-doubts—I had to find the good and make it shine. I just had to reposition my strengths to salvage this million-dollar deal.

If you are thin-skinned or prone to feeling victimized by every setback, you are limited in your potential for success. A good salesperson automatically looks for the advantage in every situation.

My strength in this situation was that I had put the whole thing together to begin with. I argued that in the best-case scenario, Briggs had had an asthma attack and an off night, but would still rise to be one of the greats in the future. I also emphasized the fact that I had gotten my fighter widespread publicity in every major newspaper and features on sports channels and could do the same for other athletes in other sports as well.

When adversity hits, remember this sage advice: Life's not fair. Get over it and feel confident that over the course of your life, things will balance out. Sometimes you win; sometimes you lose. That's just the way the world works.

Everybody faces adversity, so when it comes knocking, welcome it as a friend. Learn from it. Use it to test your character and mental strength. After all, if you save your supply of enthusiasm, ambition, and persistence only for the good times, what's the big deal? Anybody can do that. It's adversity that separates those who are all talk from those who have the heart to persist with optimism.

Critical life lessons

✓ Adversity is a fact of life. You can't avoid it or ignore it.

✓ In every moment of adversity, look for the lesson that will put you on top the next time.

✓ You lose a fight only when you refuse to get back up.

✓ There is a positive side to everything—your job is to find it.

✓ Life is a large classroom. When the lessons are expensive, think of it as the cost of knowledge.

✓ Before you financially back anything, check out the character and talent of the people behind it.

✓ Respect the promises you make, or you will create your own hole of adversity.

✓ Life is not fair. Accept it and get over it.

Network Smart

Everybody likes to say they network. They join service and community clubs; they socialize in all the right places; they trade business cards like 10-year-old kids with a new stack of baseball cards. But meeting people is not networking. Networking is all about what you do after *you meet people.*

"Networking" has become a popular buzz word in business. Its reputation promises that it is the magic key that will open doors and guarantee success. But, as many disillusioned networkers have discovered, it really is just a word. Without some know-how and direction behind it, simply joining clubs and saying "hi" to everyone is not a sure ticket to anywhere. Networking is an art; it's a skill; it's an invaluable piece of the whole picture of success—*if* you know what you're doing.

Greetings!: Indirect networking

When my boxers fight, the promoters can count on selling $300,000 to $400,000 worth of tickets. That's more tickets than any other boxing manager I know could sell, and I wouldn't be able to do it if it weren't for indirect networking.

As a sports agent, first I want to network with the people who go to athletic events. I want to know where they live, what they do, what kind of shows they go to, how often they go. But I can't get this information by just walking around shaking hands. So I asked myself how I could network with thousands of people at one time. The method I use today is the same one I started using when I was 19 years old: I hire pretty girls to go out into the audience and hand out short information surveys. To make sure I get a good response, I offer incentives to both the girls and the fans. I offer extra money (maybe an extra hundred) to the girl who gets the most cards filled out, and I offer the fans who fill out a card a chance to win a great raffle prize (maybe a TV or tickets to another event). This way, everybody is falling over themselves to give me the information I want.

Every name goes on my master list of contacts. I have about 15,000 people on this list who get my mailings about major events. They receive fliers, announcements, and newspaper and magazine clippings. I make sure we stay in touch. Even though I've never met these people and I've never spoken to them, they are important to me and I will network with them like crazy to promote my business.

The key to indirect networking is staying in touch. Just getting the names of people you've never personally met is not effective if you don't eventually make contact.

Indirect networking isn't something you can do in your spare time; it requires time and attention. I've hired a networking team that uses the mail, phone, and fax to keep all my contacts informed. The objective is to keep my customers up-to-date and interested in what I'm doing—all the time.

From my master list I have pulled out about 2,000 names that I've put on my fax list. These people get a constant flow of articles that are printed about the company, or me, or the players, or an event. Once you get people excited about your product, once they know about it and are interested in it, you won't have trouble selling it.

This contact is followed up with phone calls. That's how I get so many people at my events. When we call, these people know who we are because they receive so much information from us. They're open to our call because they're already genuinely interested in our athletes. I call the people on my networking roster and give them exciting inside information and then invite them to come to the event. I've never even met these people—but they know me, they know my company, and they come.

Networking is work—hard work. After you contact someone, the work is just beginning. Successful networking brings you in contact with people again and again and again.

Let's do lunch: Priority networking

Priority networking is very important to my business. This personal networking is done by taking people out to dinner, visiting their home or office, and sending them token gifts, for instance. Naturally, priority networking keeps me in touch with a much smaller group of people than the group on my indirect-networking list. Realistically, there are only 24 hours in a day, so I have to prioritize important customers and investors with whom I can meet directly. From the master list of 15,000, I identify those to whom I will give my personal time.

I go over my networking lists every couple of months to see who I should give more attention to, who I should shift from my top priority list to my master list or vice versa. I need to know if there's anyone I've neglected or anyone I'm giving too much of my time to who has been unreliable or has not returned phone calls. Because the priority list contains a limited number of people, I have to make sure they are the right ones.

There have been many times over the years when priority networking really worked great for me. In one recent case, I would have been stuck with a great fight and no place to put it if I hadn't networked directly with the right people at the right time.

The 1997 George Foreman vs. Shannon Briggs fight was originally scheduled to be held at the Foxwood Casino in Connecticut. Before I signed the contract for that fight, though, I had another fight scheduled at Foxwood for Tracy Paterson. I got to the Paterson fight two hours before the match was scheduled to start and I went down to the locker room to see my fighter. A guy from the casino told me I couldn't go into the locker room without a license. What? I'd been doing this for 20 years now and I had never heard of a manager needing a license to see his fighter. I got in touch with the commissioner and asked him what was going on. He listened to the story and then agreed that I needed a license. "Okay," I said, "license me now. What do I have to do?" "I can't," he said. "You have to be here two days before the fight to get a license. If you weren't here then, you must not care very much about your fighter anyway. You can't see him now."

Obviously, I wasn't going to win this one, but I still intended to come out ahead. "Ya know what?" I asked the guy from the casino, feeling really angry now. "You're supposed to have the biggest fight you've ever had here with Foreman and Briggs—well you just lost that fight. I'm taking it somewhere else." The guy looked shocked; he had just blown the biggest deal that casino ever had.

I had become very close to Mitchell Modell, the owner of Modell's Sporting Goods. One day, we went to a Yankee game together. A few innings into the game, I told him about the Foxwood fiasco. He said, "Hey, I've got a front row seat reserved behind homeplate right next to Donald Trump. Go down there and talk with him about doing the fight in one of his casinos in Atlantic City. You've got four innings to make the deal. Go!" See how this priority networking works? Mitch Modell had become one of my best friends and within six months, he was referring me to a big player who could get me out of a jam.

I went down and found my seat next to Trump and New York's Governor George Pataki. It was a great game, and business-wise, things couldn't have worked out better—by the seventh inning, Trump had agreed to pay a million bucks to do the fight. You can't begin to imagine how a relationship may benefit you down the road.

When you network with important people, use eye contact to your advantage. I know everybody says that, but few really do it. When you meet someone and shake hands, look that person right in the eye. When you talk with someone and want to make an important point, look into his or her eyes. Starting today, the next time you talk to people who are really important to you, look them right in the eye. Afterward, ask yourself if you think it made a difference. I guarantee it will.

Person to person: Chain-link networking

When I meet a person, I don't look just at what he does and how that can help me; I want to know who that person knows. In conversation and small-talk, I'll always ask who his friends are and what they do. I figure the people I meet (especially people in high places) have a whole network of their own—I want to tap into that network. I want to know the key people they know. If I meet one investor, I look at it as if I then have access to 10 other potential investors, because I'm going to try to tap into the top 10 wealthiest people that one investor knows. If I do a good job for people by keeping my promises and by keeping them informed about the organization, I get to know them and then I get to know their friends. If they're happy with what I'm doing, they will tell more potential investors and bring them around to dinners and sporting events.

No matter what business you're in, always do right by your clients. This will allow you to tap into their whole network of contacts.

My greatest supporter and backer of all time is Harvey Silverman, the senior managing director of a brokerage firm on the New York Stock Exchange called Spear, Leeds & Kellogg. (In its October 20, 1997 issue, *Investment Dealer's Digest* said that this firm controls more inventory in equities and options than any other market-making firm.) Without Harvey, I don't know where I'd be today—he put a lot of money into me when I was just starting out. But more important, he had faith in me when I was no more than a strange voice on the other end of the phone doing some desperate chain-link networking.

When I was first starting to raise money back in 1987 to support my Triple Threat boxers, I tried chain-link networking. I called everybody I knew and asked them who they knew who might have money to invest. I asked my best friend from college, Jay Levy, to give me some phone numbers. I wanted a list of everybody he knew, and his father knew, and his mother knew. Finally, I asked for his brother's number. "My brother," he said, "goes to Syracuse University and doesn't have a dime. But I think he has a fraternity brother who loves boxing and maybe has some money. I'll call my brother and ask." Great! My first contact with somebody who actually liked the sport!

The kid at Syracuse told Jay, "Yeah, I love boxing, but I don't have any money. Tell Roberts to call my dad, Harvey Silverman." What a break—somebody I knew, knew somebody, who knew somebody who said to give his dad a call! In a second, I was on the phone with Harvey Silverman even though I didn't know what, if anything, he had to invest. I gave him my enthusiastic spiel about my plans to revolutionize boxing. I mapped out all the things I would do to protect his money. I used every tactic I could think of. After about 15 minutes, he said, "You know, I love taking my son to fights. We really have a good time. So I'm going to help you out, even though I'll probably lose all my money. I'll send you a check for $60,000." And he did.

It wasn't until about two years later that I learned who Harvey Silverman really was. It turns out I had hooked up with one of the most prestigious guys on Wall Street by accident—well not really by accident. That's the thing about chain-link networking: Nothing's really an accident when you're willing to call everybody you know, ask them who they know, and then follow up on every lead you're given. When my friend Jay gave me leads to his mother and father, I didn't stop. I wanted to know about his brother. Sure his brother was in college and didn't have any money, but who did he know? Then when Harvey's son turned down the idea, I could have dropped it. A lot of people wouldn't have called a stranger's father out of the blue to ask for money. But that's how chain-link networking works—you can't drop one of the links.

The best time to talk to people with whom you want to network is after business hours when you can offer a relaxing time with good food, laughs, and fun. When you contact people in the middle of the day, they're doing 50 other things; you're not going to get their ear. Use that time to make the appointments for their quality time later.

Reciprocal networking

There will be lots of times when the people with whom you network know somebody you want to know, but they don't have the time or the interest to introduce you. When that happens, you have to take care of those people and give them a reason to take care of you. When the relationship is mutually beneficial, I call it reciprocal networking.

It was reciprocal networking that brought Joel Segal (who is now head of my football division) into my company. I first heard about Joel through a financial planner who works specifically with athletes—somebody who I knew would be of value to me. I'd kept in touch with the guy for about 15 years and always let him know what I was doing. One day he suggested that if I ever wanted to get into football, I should contact this football agent he knew named Joel Segal.

Joel had a lot of big names in football on his roster and had a great reputation for working really hard and being honest. But I could tell he hadn't peaked just yet. At that time, Joel worked out of his house; he didn't have a fax machine, a beeper, or a cellular phone. He wasn't doing nearly what I knew he could do.

I really worked hard to bring Joel over. I kept telling him that I could give him the tools he needed to build his business, that I could enhance his career, that he could be in on the first public all-sports company, that he would benefit from my connections. He wasn't biting. Direct networking had put me in touch with Joel, but that wasn't enough.

One day, I was telling another friend of mine the story about the agent I couldn't get. He said, "I have a fraternity brother who's an agent, maybe you'd like to talk to him." Because I had run out of enticements for Segal, I was ready to move on. My friend said, "His name is Joel Segal; I'll give you his number." Bingo! You just never know when the old "somebody-who-knows-somebody" is going to kick in. Now I knew two people who knew Segal. But still, this wasn't enough—I needed them to speak to Joel for me. And I knew that with the possible business connections that could be made for all of us, they wouldn't mind talking to Segal for me.

I have an advantage in reciprocal networking—people like to be around my celebrity athletes. But in any business, you have to use whatever you have to your advantage. Everybody has something good to offer. If you work for a cookie company, there are lots of people who'd like to see how cookies are made and would like to bring a few boxes home to the family. If you make window blinds, you can offer free advice from an interior decorator. Offer something to get something.

Up to this point, Segal had no way of knowing if I was just another fast-talker in this business (there are a few). Now he had two people he trusted telling him I was honest and hard-working and was offering him a legitimate opportunity.

Reciprocal networking usually works: On my own, I had worked on Joel for almost a year with no progress; with the help of two other people who had common business interests, I had him two months later.

Take good care of the people with whom you network. Then give them a reason to take care of you.

Heads up: On-the-spot networking

I'm always looking for people to network with. I plan out networking strategies and position myself to be in the right place at the right time. But sometimes networking happens when you least expect it. That's why you always have to be prepared!

After the Super Bowl in 1998, my marketing manager, Ryan Schinman, packed a hundred or so business cards in his pocket and headed off to the parties. He had no idea exactly who was going to be there, but he knew there'd be top corporate people all over the place and he wanted to be ready for anyone who could give him a good deal for our Packers player, Antonio Freeman. By the end of the evening, Ryan had pocketed three major deals for Freeman. Antonio was picked up as a pitchman for QVC cable shopping network, hired by EA Sports to give input in the making of their football video games, and picked up for the Packers' signing tour. Not a bad night of on-the-spot networking.

Opportunities for networking happen every time you walk out the door. You've got to be ready to work deals on the spot.

Moving on: Dead-end networking

Successful networking is time-consuming. It's easy to get a business card and put people in your computer file, but it takes time to keep in touch. You have to call. You have to get together. You have to sacrifice business and personal time to make it work. That's why it's important to carefully identify the people you will give most of your networking time to and which ones you won't.

Networking is like any decision in life: You have to make the right choices. Otherwise, you'll put an awful lot of time into people who don't have the time, power, or ability to do anything good for you.

In the financial world, networking is all-important. When you're dealing with money, you want to know who can get hot deals and who has the best and most up-to-date information. You've got to network to get this information, but you have to be careful whom you network with.

I once met a guy who was with a financial firm that was in on a really big deal; I thought he could do good things for me. I took him out for 15 or 20 dinners; I went to his house on weekends and I got to know his wife and kids; I sent him all kinds of sports memorabilia. I really invested myself in our relationship. I thought I was a shoo-in to get a huge allocation.

It turns out this guy didn't have the ability to give me anything. I didn't do my homework to find out if he had the power I thought he had. I spent a lot of time that could have been used to network with somebody else who had the ability and power to help me. It may sound crass to say that I wasted time building a relationship, but that's a fact of networking.

There isn't a successful businessperson in the world who doesn't build relationships purely for personal benefit. I don't mean I don't make friends along the way, too, but I have to weigh how much time I can spend with people based on how much they can offer my company—that's business.

Network with attitude

Whatever kind of networking you choose to do, the results are all a matter of attitude. When you talk to people, perk up! Always say, "Things are great today!" Make it seem like things are great even when the sky is falling. If you're a salesperson, let everybody know you just sold 500 refrigerators (there's no need to mention the other thousand sitting in the warehouse costing you a fortune). When good things happen, spread the word. Tell people, "I'm so excited because I'm getting the national sales award!" Don't be shy about your accomplishments. People like to do business with winners.

No matter what's going on, don't moan. The people you really want to network with are heavy hitters who hear enough moaning and complaining from their own people. They don't want to hear it from you, too. If you're an accountant, don't complain during tax season about being busy. Turn it around to sound terrific: "Man, I've got so many clients. I can't believe how many people want to trust me with their finances."

Focus all your conversations on the good things that have happened in your business and in your life.

Networking isn't being pushy—as long as you're charming about it. Most people like to hear from me, not because of me, but because they want to know how my athletes are doing. They like to hear from me because they know I'll be upbeat and positive. I've always got good news to share. People don't mind a friendly voice giving them information they're interested in.

It's your job to create an aura about you that will make people happy to hear from you and want to be around you. People always want to be with other people who have enthusiasm and a love for life. Make sure that when you call someone that person hears a lively, upbeat voice on the other end of the phone. Make people laugh. Make them want to talk with you.

I couldn't stay in business if I didn't dedicate so much of my time to networking. I found out very early that who you know in life really does make a difference. There's still no doubt in my mind that determination, perseverance, enthusiasm, and a positive attitude are the backbone of success. But careful and persistent networking give those personal attributes the boost and support they need to be effective in this very competitive world.

Critical life lessons

✓ Networking is more than just exchanging business cards. Successful networking depends on what you do *after* you meet people.

✓ Don't overlook the value of indirect networking. It puts you in contact with thousands of people you've never even met.

✓ Marketing strategies, such as direct mail and telemarketing, are all part of savvy networking.

✓ Choose carefully the people you will give your personal time to. There aren't enough hours in the day to wine and dine everyone you meet.

✓ Making a great contact through networking is only the beginning. Make sure you tap into that person's own network of friends and colleagues.

✓ Networking is mutually beneficial if you can offer something to get something.

✓ You will save yourself time and money if you carefully identify the people you will give most of your networking time to.

✓ People are naturally attracted to upbeat, positive individuals. Smile, be happy, and get yourself out there.

Match the Person to the Job

Employees are valuable assets, especially in a people business like mine. They have to be chosen with care and nurtured. Whether you're the one doing the hiring or the one being hired, a good match between the job and the applicant is vital—a mismatched employee is a miserable employee and is bad for business.

There's nothing worse than having a mismatch between an employee and a job. The employee is unhappy, the job doesn't get done with care, and the customers are angry and disappointed. Everybody loses in the end. If you're interviewing candidates for a job opening, or if you're the candidate, take time to choose wisely.

Costly mistakes

Finding a good match between employee and job is important to the success of any business. This is not a step to take lightly.

When you're doing the hiring

A stable work force lets you focus on your product or service and your customers instead of recruiting, orienting, training, and developing new employees. If you make a mistake in the hiring process, you've got major problems:

- ✓ In today's litigious world, you can't fire someone without risking a lawsuit (especially if *you* made the mistake in the hiring process).
- ✓ You and your company can also be sued if you do not use what the law calls "due diligence" during the hiring process, and you end up with an employee who harms others or destroys property.

✓ If you hire the wrong person and he or she eventually quits, you're stuck with the exorbitant cost of employee turnover. These costs include separation or severance pay, the cost of attracting new applicants, the cost of filling the void with overtime and temporary help until a new employee is found, the cost of conducting interviews and ordering background checks, the cost of new training, and the cost due to lost productivity during the transition period.

✓ The cost of bad hiring comes not just from crimes, such as embezzlement, but from the loss of customers, productivity, profits, reputation, and sometimes lawsuits. It also comes from the loss of company secrets that fly to your competitors when employees are lured away.

When you're doing the job hunting

If you land in a job that's not right for you, it will cost you:

✓ You'll lose a lot of time that could have gone into career building.

✓ You'll spend effort going in the wrong direction.

✓ You'll lose motivation and ambition.

✓ You'll end up being either just one of the thousands of people who spend a lifetime in jobs they hate, or you'll end up back at square one in the job market.

Save yourself this misery and choose right the first time.

Poor job matching isn't a mere inconvenience. It is a major obstacle to career and business success.

Think before you jump

Hiring a new employee or taking a new job is a big step. You've got to give the process your time and attention *before* you find yourself at an interview. If you think ahead about what you're looking for, you're more likely to find it.

When you're doing the hiring

Know your business. Think about exactly what you want before you go looking. What kind of person do you need? What skills? What philosophy? What goals? These are things you need to know before you even start looking for an employee.

First, determine what credentials, schooling, and/or experience this person must have. These are the things you should decide on in advance and things you can't compromise on. These are the things that help you screen applicants right from their resumes. I want the heads of my basketball and football divisions to be lawyers. That's the credential that these positions require, so only lawyers are even considered. Why waste anybody's time giving interviews to people without the bottom-line requirements?

Next, you should think about the *type* of person you're looking for. I like to make sure that my employees' philosophies conform with my own. You need a clear understanding of the personality and attitude you're looking for. These are things that can be more important than specific skills. If the person has the right credentials and the right attitude, you can teach him or her anything.

Finally, you need to evaluate the life style that fits the position. In the sports business, I need people in key positions who are free to work round the clock. When we're recruiting athletes and there's a prospect we need to speak to right away, I need recruiters who can jump on a plane any day of the week and stay on the job for as long as it takes. I can call any one of my recruiters right now and say, "There's a kid out in Minnesota you have to talk to today," and that recruiter will be out there on the next flight. Not everybody can do this. People who can't do this aren't bad employees; they're just not cut out to be *my* employees. Knowing this in advance helps me know what questions to ask at an interview and lets me be up front with candidates. I don't want to hire somebody and then say, "Oh, didn't I tell you? This job involves lots of travel and time away from home." You end up with employees who don't fit the job, and that's bad for the employees, and it's bad for your business.

Know yourself. There are certain things that you probably feel are important to have in key employees. Taking the time to figure out what these things are will help you find people who fit in well with the goals of your company. I know exactly what I like to see in a new employee. I look for people who can take direction, people I can guide. The sports business is full of people with big egos—they can all go work somewhere else. I get turned off by people who think they know it all already. Of course experience is a great thing, but every business is different in its approach and philosophy. If I hire a recruiter who's been in this business for 15 years, I still want that person to be open to learning how we work and how we reach our company goals.

I also look for people who will appreciate what I give them. I give my employees all the weapons they can possibly need to do the best job. But I want to know that they appreciate that, because appreciation builds loyalty. In any business, the best employees are always being lured away by competitors. I need employees who recognize that I give them more than they can get anywhere else and who appreciate that fact. Before I go into an interview, I know these are things I'll be looking for in attitude and personality.

When you're doing the job hunting

Know the requirements of the job. You should know in advance the responsibilities of the job to make sure the position is right for you. Take a good look at the job and be honest with yourself. If you don't want to travel or work overtime, for example, don't apply for jobs that will require these things. So many people figure that they'll put up with things they hate just to get their foot in the door and then they'll switch to a different position and do the things they like. That's usually a poor plan. If you hate what you're doing, it's very unlikely you'll do it well enough and with the right attitude to move into a better position.

Know yourself. What circumstances are most motivating for you? What kind of job will make you want to get out there every day and work your hardest? If you love to work with people and move around, why even look at a job that would put you in a cubicle with a calculator? If you are a great team player who feeds off the enthusiasm of others, stay away from jobs that send you out on your own. If you have the entrepreneurial spirit, you can skip over jobs that are confining and micromanaged. Before you apply for any position, be honest with yourself about your personal needs and strengths. These will guide you to the right position.

Some pre-employment soul-searching is necessary to figure out what you want and need before you jump into action.

Determining the right type of employment

Nine-to-5 is not the only type of employment out there. Be flexible in your thinking before making a final decision.

When you're doing the hiring

When you have a position to fill, think over your options about the different types of employees you can hire. Do you need a full-time employee, a part-time employee, a temporary employee, or an independent contractor?

Full-time and part-time employees. You can decide if you want a full-time or a part-time employee based on the amount of work you need done. This is an obvious consideration that a lot of employers overlook. Don't automatically jump into full-time help if part-time is what you need.

Temporary help. I don't use temporary help. First of all, there's no way I can build loyalty in these employees and I can't match their work philosophies to the company's. Also, because they're here today, gone tomorrow, they don't service my clients and customers the way regular employees do. This isn't their fault—it's the nature of the position.

In other businesses, temporary employees might be necessary. If you have a rush of business during seasonal times of the year, for example, a temp may be the only sound economic move you can make. Another good reason to use temps is related to losing customers. If you feel you would lose more customers who have to wait for service than those who get poor or untrained service, then having a temp serve your customers would be better than having no one serve them. The key is to know your customers' needs and decide if a temp can meet those needs.

Independent contractors. Independent contractors are hired on a temporary basis to handle specialized functions or tasks that your own personnel cannot do. You may send the work outside the business to be done off premises. Or you may hire an individual to come into your company to work on a particular project until it's done. You pay this person a specific fee for the job; you do not pay for sick days; you do not give medical benefits or cover social security or unemployment insurance.

Because the government has made it tougher to hire independent contractors, I've been staying away from this type of employee. If I hire an independent "consultant" to work *exclusively* on my project, the government says he or she is my employee—not a contractor. But if I hire a consultant who takes my project on as just one of many, I have no way of knowing how much attention he or she is giving to me. I want people who focus on my needs. I want all my employees to care about my business and its success. I don't think I can get this from a "consultant" who works for many other people at the same time.

Take a pencil and paper and figure out if hiring an independent contractor is right for you. You have to weigh the economics of the arrangement and determine if you need that person's complete attention all day long. If you want someone who will focus exclusively on your project, then you shouldn't hire an independent contractor. But a contractor may be the best choice if your goal is to get a talented person who can get the job done right the first time and then be gone, and at the same time save yourself the cost of payroll employees.

You have to analyze what you're trying to accomplish. If you want exclusive attention and work that you can supervise, you have to go with a payroll employee. But if you want to save some money, don't care if the contractor has lots of other things going on at the same time, and it's okay that you can't directly supervise the work, then an independent contractor may be perfect.

When you're doing the job hunting

Before you hit the job market with resume in hand, take some time to think about the type of employee you want to be. In this world of "flexible" employment, you have a lot of options that you should consider before assuming that a full-time, 9-to-5 position is best. Think about full-time versus part-time. Look into temporary services that give you the chance to "try out" a field or position before making a contract commitment. And think about the ever-popular "consulting" industry. Independent, freelance contractors have become a big thing recently. If you have a skill that you can market to many different companies, and you have an entrepreneurial spirit, independent contracting may be for you. My advice is to think over your options carefully before blindly landing in a place that's not right for you.

Compensation

An underpaid employee is an unhappy employee who won't give 100 percent or stay with the company for very long. Before you finalize a job offer, take time to make sure the compensation matches the job.

When you're doing the hiring

Before you advertise to fill a job, decide how much that position is worth to you. I work on the belief that if I pay my employees very well, they'll pay me back in loyalty and service. It's my experience that if you want the people who work for you to give their full attention to the job, you have to make sure they have enough money to live.

I make sure my key people have nice homes, two good cars, and a six-figure income. They don't wake up in the morning and worry about how they're going to pay the mortgage. If employees are distracted by financial worries, their performance, and then the profits of my company, will definitely be affected. My employees can stay motivated to work because they have clear heads. They don't ever have to think about taking a second job. This alleviates the pressures of paying bills. They can concentrate on meeting their goals. The only thing they have to worry about is being the best they can be. With clear heads, they have all the opportunity in the world to become very wealthy. I want to know what they need to reduce their financial pressures so they can be at the top of their game. The extra focus that financial security gives them makes them 10 times more productive and gets 10 times better results. This gives me a much better bottom line. I take that and package it up and sell it to Wall Street. This brings in more investors. Skimping on payroll is foolish.

Compensation isn't only money. Think about what kind of package you can put together to attract and keep the best in the business. Decide if you will offer incentives, such as car allowances, travel expenses, entertainment allowances, educational benefits, stock options, or profit sharing. These things can be equally or even more important than salary.

When you're doing the job hunting

After you objectively evaluate your credentials and your experience, ask yourself, "How much am I worth? Realistically, can I earn that?" The answers to these questions should guide your job search. If you hold out for the six-figure income when you've got two years' experience and no special training in the field, you'll be unemployed for a long time. On the other hand, if you're skilled and experienced, but you take a job where you're underpaid, you'll be unhappily employed for a long time.

Evaluate your value in the marketplace. Find out what other people with your credentials are making. Find out what companies in your area who employ for similar positions are paying. Run through the classifieds to get an idea of what's being offered. Contact business associations, such as trade organizations or the local chamber of commerce, for hiring statistics. Then apply only to those jobs that will adequately reward what you bring to the company.

Throwing out the bait

If you want to put yourself ahead of the pack rushing to fill the same positions, think creatively about where to look for the best. The effort it takes to look past the classifieds into more intensive recruiting areas is well worth it in the end.

When you're doing the hiring

In my business it's easy to find job candidates. We're a popular, high-profile industry, and people send us resumes all day long. But if I needed to go looking for applicants, I know how I'd do it. I would:

✓ Avoid classified ads. Getting applications from such a mass market makes it too difficult and time-consuming to weed out the quality applicants.

✓ Use referrals. I'd much rather interview someone who has been recommended by a mutual acquaintance than someone coming in cold.

✓ Start with the local colleges. Get to know the deans in the departments with majors related to your business. The deans know the top students and they can refer you to the best. If you're looking for a secretary, go to secretarial schools. If you're looking for a computer programmer, go to the computer training schools. Ask to interview the top five students in the class.

✓ Raid successful competitors. This is the place where you'll find your most experienced people who already know how the industry works. Of course, you have to offer them incentives to leave and come to you (things such as money, stock, power, position), but if you want them, it's worth it. If you're a small company raiding a big company, use that to your advantage by offering opportunities for a quick climb to the top that isn't possible in the big company. If you're the big company raiding a small company, you can offer prestige, status, and money.

✓ Use online resources. You can create your own Web page to describe your company and list your employment needs. Or you can review resumes posted on the Internet by applicants seeking employment in your field. There are many ways to find these resumes; you can start by typing in your request. I might search for "sports agent seeking employment," for example. Or you can visit employment sites, such as America's Job Bank (www.ajb.dni.us/index.html) or TOPjobs USA™ (www.topjobsusa.com).

✓ Try head hunters. When you're hiring for a highly specialized position and have exhausted other avenues, this is the way to go. They can be the pit-bulls you need to bring in the best.

✓ Hire interns. Interns are the best. They're enthusiastic; they're hard workers; they've got lots of energy; they take direction; and they work for free. We've had interns who were top of their class out of schools like Princeton and Harvard who have been great assets to our company. No matter what business you're in, go to your local colleges and ask for interns. It's like getting to try out a future employee without any obligation. This is an all-win-can't-lose situation. You can't beat interns.

When I decided to expand my company beyond boxing, I knew I needed to hire a marketing director. Because mine was a new company and I hadn't hired anyone for this position before, I didn't want to get someone who needed training or hand-holding, so I went right to my competitors and took one of their best—Ryan Schinman. Ryan was assistant marketing director and head of the football division for a company called Athletes and Artists (now Marquee Group). I wanted a young agent with good connections in the business who would be around for a long time—Ryan fit this description (plus his employer had given him four years of top training). When we contacted him, he was very happy at his job and had no intentions of leaving. But as we met over the next two months through business meetings and social get-togethers, he found out that our vision for the future was so similar to his and the opportunities at my company were so wide open that he couldn't resist. I remember telling Ryan that because he was a young man (only about 24 at the time), this was the time to take a chance. (I knew this was a risk for him to jump from an established company with 20 years in the business to my company, which at that time had just three boxers.) I also encouraged him to leave the door open at Athletes and Artists in case he changed his mind. The challenge was to convince Ryan that this was not a sprint I was asking him to run; it was a marathon. I was in this for the long haul and I needed other people who thought they could go the distance.

When you're doing the job hunting

When you're looking for a job, think like an employer. Where would an employer like to find the best employee? The section above, as well as the tips that follow, should give you a hint.

✓ Stay away from the classifieds if possible; it's too easy to get lost in the crowd.

✓ Try to get a mutual acquaintance to give you an introduction or a referral.

✓ If you're in college or a training school, get to know the dean and department heads. Ask them for referrals.

✓ If you're looking for a new job in the same field, target competitors. Your experience is valuable to them.

✓ Look for companies that hire interns. Internships are no longer only for college kids. Many of the top companies have internships for adults with experience. It's annoying to have to work for free for a while, but it's a way to get in the door and show off what you can do. Consider it an apprenticeship.

The interview

By the time you get to the interview, you should be pretty sure that you've made a good match between what you want and what the job requires.

When you're doing the hiring

Know the skills you need. On the first round of an interview, jump right on the skills that the employee needs to have. If you need somebody who is a computer whiz or a cold-call magician, go right to those points first. The resume that highlights the needed skills gets candidates in the door, but it's the interview that sifts out the people who really know what they're doing from those who don't.

Know the needs of the other employees. If the person you're hiring is going to be working with other people, you have to make sure the new person will fit in. You can bring in the most talented employee, but if he or she can't stand being in the same room with your other employees, you've got a disaster on your hands. I figure getting the right team of employees is like putting together a basketball team. You can have the best talent, like Michael Jordan and Scottie

Pippen, but if they don't like each other, they're not going to play well together.

If the new employee is going to work under or be an equal partner with someone else, you have to make sure these two people think the same and can get along. I bring in the person they're going to work with right into the interview and let them meet, talk, and share experiences. Once I've got a good idea of who I'd like to hire, I want that person to hang out with his or her supervisor or partner for a week or two—maybe go out to dinner, go see a client, or spend some time on the job. This gives the current employee a chance to decide if he or she can work with the new employee. And it gives the new employee a chance to loosen up and offer a true picture of his or her personality and work ethic.

Know the personality you need. Here's where you can try to match your personal philosophies with those of the applicant. To do this, I ask questions like: "What are your goals?" "What are your objectives and how do you plan to meet them?" You need a clear understanding of where that person's head is at.

I need my employees to be team players, not all "stars." So I listen very carefully to the way candidates describe their experience. If their stories are full of: "*I* did this. *I* did that," that's a warning sign to me. In my company, "*We* do this and *we* do that." That's the attitude all my employees have to have if we're going to accomplish our company goals.

I also look for an indication that a person will be loyal. The last thing I want is to bring people in, back them, teach them, move them into key positions, and then have them leave. This is an instinctive call because there's nothing on a resume that will guarantee loyalty, but the right kind of interview will usually give me enough to make an "educated" gut evaluation.

When I'm hiring, the "right" kind of interview doesn't follow a strict format of rigid questions and answers. I like to talk and relax. I like to take the top candidates out to dinner, get them to loosen up. I want to see their personalities and their makeup. I get the facts about background and experience from their resumes and first-round interviews, then I want to get to know them as people.

The interview is like business socializing. It's a time to get a good grasp of what you need to know while at the same time making the other person feel relaxed and at ease.

When you're doing the job hunting

Know the skills you need. Don't waste everybody's time by applying for jobs that you don't have experience or credentials for. Some people think that they can talk their way in the door. Maybe they can, but it's hard to shine in a position you're not fit for. I think I'd rather give my attention and energy to positions where I know I'm the best and can show my competence quickly.

Know the needs of the interviewer. When you're being interviewed for a job, you have to know what the interviewer is thinking. If I were being interviewed for a job, I'd want the interviewer to know we're compatible. I'd size up what he or she likes and make sure it's known that I like that, too. I'd want to present myself as a team player. I'd ask, "Who will I be working with? I'd love to meet them. Do you think it would be a good idea for us to get together?" I'd hope to have an opportunity to interact with these people so they could go back to the boss and relate how ambitious I am and how much I want the job.

Know the company philosophy. Some companies look for people with an entrepreneurial spirit who need no supervision. Others look for team players who follow direction well. Some want people who put the company first in their lives. Others want 9-to-5ers who don't expect too much in return. If at all possible before an interview, find out the company philosophies. Talk to people who work there. Strike up a conversation with the receptionist. Your chances of getting the job are much better if your attitude and philosophy match those of the interviewer.

Know yourself. If you have faith in your own ability to do the job, offer to work on a trial basis. Tell the interviewer, "I'm so sure you'll like the way I work that I'm willing to work the first week for free. If you're still not sure if you want to hire me, I'll work another week for free. After that week you'll have no doubt that I'm the best one for the job." What do you have to lose? If you don't get the job, chances are you would have been sitting around at home those two weeks anyway!

Background checks

Background checks are just a fact of life. If you're doing the hiring, schedule them right into your recruitment plan. If you're applying for a job, expect to be checked out.

When you're doing the hiring

Your first line of information about an applicant comes from the resume and/or application. Don't make the mistake of assuming that what you read in these documents is necessarily so. It has become common sport to "punch up" one's credentials—in other words: Lie. If a credential or experience is vital to job performance, check the facts. Call colleges and training schools, call former employers. You'll be surprised how often the facts don't match.

Always check references. For some reason, people think you're not really going to call their references, but that's crazy. What does it take? Five minutes to find out where they come from and how they did there? Make reference checks a top priority before you make any job offer. If a resume says, "References available upon request," request them! You can save a lot of time, effort, and money if you find out up front that this is a person with a bad work history. I like to ask for four references. I figure I'll probably talk to the person's best friends on the first two, but by the fourth, I should be getting a true picture of the person.

It's also worth it to spend some money on professional background checks to make sure potential employees are fit for the job. This is especially important for employees who will go out and meet clients and represent the company. Background checks usually include a person's criminal history, credit rating, and driving record. They can also confirm employment, education, and licensing. This information helps you find qualified employees, but it also protects you legally. It sounds crazy, but if you hire an employee who (unknown to you) has a record, let's say for breaking and entering, and that employee delivers your product to a customer's home, and then goes back after work and robs that home—you can be held liable for negligent hiring. The same goes for a driver with a DWI violation who is hired and then injures someone in a car accident after a liquid lunch. You can also be held liable if an employee with an assault conviction turns on a fellow employee and beats the heck out of him. You can even be held liable if you place an employee with a bad credit history in front of a cash register.

Today's laws make it absolutely necessary to apply "due diligence" in all business decisions. Remember the case of John Spano? Spano got the backing to buy a National Hockey League franchise, the New York Islanders, for $165 million by claiming assets of $250 million in Treasury bills and off-shore accounts. He received loans of $8 million from a Dallas bank and $80 million from a Boston bank. It all fell apart when Spano failed to meet a $16.8 million installment payment for the team and pleaded guilty to fraud. It was then reported in court that his assets totaled barely more than $1 million. It was the NHL who was guilty of conducting only a cursory investigation of Spano's assets before approving his purchase of the team. These "due diligence" laws make it mandatory for you to do your homework before you make any business decision—including hiring a new employee.

Much of the information you need is public record and is available to anyone, but it is smart business to hire a professional who can do the job quickly, thoroughly, professionally, and legally. Security companies, private investigators, employment screening companies are all listed in the yellow pages of the phone book.

You might also want to look into applicant testing. These tests cover a wide range of areas, including drug and alcohol testing, physical exams, integrity testing, values evaluations, behavioral-style evaluations, and job skills tests. To decide which tests will help you find the best employees, you should consult an employment specialist who is knowledgeable in the law, uses of pre-employment evaluation, and the position you're trying to fill. These services are especially vital when you're looking at key positions in your company that directly affect your overall success.

When you're doing the job hunting

Background checks are a reality of our time. You can expect a prospective employer to dig deep to find out if you would fit as an employee. You can help that search go in your favor by supplying sound and knowledgeable references. Don't put down your brother and your best friend. Find someone who knows you professionally who will say nice things. In addition, you can expect that many prospective employers may require a battery of pre-employment checks and tests. When you fill out an application, look for the release statement that gives the company the right to investigate your background. Once you sign, everything about you is fair game. Prospective employers can run background checks on your criminal history, credit rating, and driving record. They can also confirm employment, education, and licensing. You can be asked to submit to certain types of tests and evaluations, which were described earlier.

I know lots of people lie on applications and resumes, but that's a mistake for a lot of reasons. Even if you don't get found out, I still think it puts you in danger of ending up somewhere you don't belong. This almost happened to me. When I was in my early 20s, I went to the William Morris Agency to get a job as a celebrity agent. I had a terrific interview that focused on my experience as a promoter and all the things I had done at such a young age. Then the interviewer asked, "Where did you go to college?" Well, I did go to college...right? so I could have lied right there, but instead I admitted that I had never graduated. The interviewer smiled. She shook my hand and said she was sure there was a place for me in the company and that she'd call me the next day. The next morning, I got a phone call that began, "You're the best candidate I've ever interviewed." She continued, "But it's a company policy that we don't hire anyone without a college education. I'm sorry." I had been honest because I thought that's always the best policy, but here honesty was unfairly slamming a door in my face. Of course, at the time, I figured I should have lied, but now looking back, it's obvious that being deceptive would have changed the course of my whole life and I probably wouldn't have ended up where I belong. When you're honest, things work out as they should.

Don't be insulted by background checks. If you have nothing to hide, you can respect the employers' need to do everything possible to find good people and to protect themselves from negligent-hiring lawsuits. If you do have something in your background that will be uncovered through one of these checks, you should bring it up yourself. At least you'll get a chance to explain yourself and offer assurances for future actions. If something that you haven't mentioned comes up on a report, you may be eliminated from consideration without that opportunity to explain.

You can also turn the tables on the availability of database information. Before you jump into a job, check out the company. Find out if the company is on steady ground. Look for signs of growth and potential. If it's a publicly traded company, find out how the stockholders feel about the future of the company. Look to see what the executives and key people are being paid and how long they've been there. All of this is public information available through computer checks, from industry references, and from the company's annual report.

Today's computer databases make fact-checking a fast and easy way to match the right applicant to the right job. Don't overlook their value.

Reeling them in

In a strong economy, finding the right match between job and employee is only the beginning. In many instances, if you're the employer, you may have to put together an enticing employment package when you make a job offer. If you're the applicant, you may have room to negotiate for a better deal.

When you're doing the hiring

Once you've screened all the applicants for basic job requirements and then interviewed the top of the bunch, it's time to make a job offer to the best candidate. If you're hiring someone right out of college, the basics of the job (hours, compensation, and benefits) should be spelled out and offered in what the candidate should perceive as a take-it-or-leave-it offer. This is standard, especially when candidates number two and three are just as qualified.

But if the candidate you want is an experienced, one-of-a-kind gem, the job offer has to be put together very carefully with room to negotiate. If you want somebody badly enough, you may have to take a risk and overpay him or her. Of course, you should start with a low offer, knowing that you'll keep going up until you make an offer he or she can't refuse. That's the risk/reward of hiring. You risk the high payout for the reward of getting an excellent, long-term employee. You should also have a pocketful of incentives that can encourage the candidate to get over that natural resistance to change.

One of my toughest hiring experiences was getting Joel Segal to join Worldwide Entertainment and Sports as head of the football division. Joel had been on his own as a successful football agent since he got out of law school and he owned and ran one of the top football agencies. I knew that Joel had turned down other offers with large sports management companies because he wanted to be on his own. But I also knew that I wanted him.

As you'll remember, I met Joel through a financial planner, Gary Scharf. But it wasn't until I passed the word of my interest in hiring him through a mutual friend that Joel reluctantly agreed to meet me at a restaurant. That night I had three tables filled with a whole group of interesting people, and I wanted Joel to join us and have a good time. That's all, no business talk, just get to know each other. Today, Joel says that he walked into that restaurant only as a courtesy and left feeling excited about the possibility of meeting me again another time—that's all I wanted out of our first meeting. It was still going to be a difficult sell because Joel didn't think he needed me. I knew differently. Because he was so independent, I decided that my goal would be to make Joel understand how much I needed him. I wanted him to feel like my company couldn't run without him. I wanted to convince Joel that the support and weapons I could give him would make him the best in the business. Joel became a priority, so I treated him like one. I sent a limo to pick him up for our meetings. I took him out to dinner many times. I introduced him to investors and brokers who were very involved in making WWES a success. I took him to sporting events. Joel sat in the front row with the VIPs at the Mercer vs. Witherspoon fight and I put him up in a palatial suite and provided every amenity he could dream of. Of course anybody with money could buy these same things, so there had to be more. I wanted Joel to see my commitment and my energy, and I wanted him to recognize that I was offering him the opportunity to do something new, exciting, and pioneering.

I know that if I can lure people in, there's no doubt in the world that they'll know after one month that it was the best decision they ever made. The key is to get them in the door. I try to leave room in the contract for an out that makes them feel better about coming in. I'll say that if she wants to leave after six months, she can with no obligations. If I want a person badly enough and I'm having trouble getting a commitment, I'll offer a $50,000 exit bonus the person can collect if she doesn't like working with me and wants to leave after six months. That gives the person the courage to leave a job and give Worldwide Entertainment and Sports a try.

When you're doing the job hunting

When a company makes you a job offer, that's the point at which they'll probably talk about salary, benefits, and perks. For some positions in some companies, there is no negotiation involved. This is the deal, take it or leave it. But unless you know that for sure, there's no harm in trying to negotiate yourself a better deal than the first one thrown on the table. (Never try to negotiate *before* the offer is made— that's a bad move.) You have to remember that by the time an offer is made, the company has already put a lot of time and money into the selection process and you've come out on top. Thank them for the offer and then be ready with your terms. It's not a good idea to ask for $25,000 more than you're offered or an additional four weeks' vacation in the first year. But within reason, raise the bar. I've never heard of anybody yanking away a job offer because the candidate tried to negotiate better terms. If the answer is no, you land where you started and still have the job.

Staying happy

I know a lot of companies have very elaborate orientation programs for new employees. Each company has to decide on the best way to keep new employees happy. Personally, I don't believe it's a good idea to do a lot of initial hand-holding. I need take-charge people who are comfortable diving into the middle of things. What they need is an equal balance of both support and autonomy. When new employees come in, they know I'm watching out for them. I'm constantly in touch, asking, "What do you need to do your job? What can I give you?" They know I'm there for them with a backbone of support. At the same time, I want them to have the independent flexibility they need to do their own thing. They should be able to pave their own road and see where it goes. Of course, if I don't like the road they're taking, we'll sit down, have a talk, and get back on track. The right combination of autonomy and support keeps most employees very happy—and it keeps them from leaving after six months and asking for their $50,000 exit bonus. (For more details about staying happy on the job, see Rule #7.)

Critical life lessons

✓ Matching the right job with the right employee is vital to personal and business success.

✓ Think about what you need personally and professionally before you jump into the job market.

✓ The smart businessperson knows not all jobs require a full-time employee. Look at the options before settling on the norm.

✓ Good pay equals good attitude and performance. There's no getting around it.

✓ The best employees and the best jobs are not usually floating near the surface of the employment pool. Dive deep to find the top.

✓ Resumes uncover the details. Interviews uncover the person.

✓ Be proactive, not reactive, on background checks—they are your legal protection against charges of negligent hiring.

✓ If there's room to negotiate a hiring offer, plan the perimeters in advance. You don't want to appear tongue-tied by a counteroffer.

✓ Successful orientation in a new job requires both support and freedom.

Get Them Psyched!

Any job in the world will get done better, faster, and more efficiently by someone who really wants to do well. Someone who loves what he does. Someone who has something to prove. Someone who is determined to be the best. These are the characteristics of a motivated person. These are the characteristics you want to nurture in all of your employees.

I know there are people out there who motivate their employees with fear and intimidation—and sometimes they get impressive bottom-line results. We've all seen coaches like that, the ones who yell, "You stink! You call yourself a ball player?" expecting to push the player to try harder. But in the long run, I don't think this motivational style works. I think it's the coach who yells encouragement and who tells that player, "Don't worry about it. Keep shooting," who will get the better results. I'd rather try to get the best out of my people by building them up than by knocking them down.

The way people work with you has a lot to do with how they feel about you. They'll feel committed to your goals and work hard if you treat them right. That's not really difficult to do—just listen to how you talk to the people around you. Tomorrow, keep track of what you say during the first hour of work. How often do you give out instructions? Compare that to how many times you ask for input. Count how often you point out problems. Compare that to how many times you comment on a job well done. In just one hour, you'll get a good picture of your management style.

If you complain more often than you compliment, make a conscious effort to change. Go out of your way to find something good to say at least twice a day. After a while, it will become a habit, and the funny thing is, the more often you compliment people, the more often they'll do terrific things.

How many times today have you said something like, "You're the best," "You're doing a great job," "You're the greatest"? Compliment your employees on the great job they're doing—this will motivate them to keep doing a great job.

Make everyone your partner

You can motivate key people in your organization by calling them partners, even if you're not a public company with shares to sell. Even before we went public, I always introduced my best people as my partners. When I'd call them on the phone, I'd say, "Hey, how's my partner?" When they'd do a good job, I'd say, "That's why you're my partner in this." The more you call people "partners" the harder they'll work, because they will begin to feel like it's their business, too. This simple tactic creates a sense of camaraderie and brings people together to work toward the same goal.

To make the people you work with feel important and valued, you sometimes have to hide your own ego. When you introduce employees to clients or customers, build them up, not yourself. Say, "This is Tom Smith. He's the best. He's the greatest."

Try to find opportunities to make your "partners" shine. I've told my public relations agent to focus not just on me, but also on members of my staff. I want them to have their names in the news, too. When one of my marketing guys was quoted in *Newsweek* in an article about the golfer Casey Martin, it was great publicity for him. This kind of name recognition makes it easier for this employee to do a good job. My people were quoted in the news during both the Marv Albert and Latrell Sprewell scandals and they're frequently on CNBC sports shows. I put my recruiters' pictures in my company brochures and I include interviews with them in our promotional videos. My job is to build up the people around me so they feel proud to work for Worldwide Entertainment and Sports. Standing in the spotlight today is a great motivator to get out there tomorrow and do even better. When you're mapping out ways to get exposure for yourself and your company, don't forget to shine some attention on your employees, too.

Really make them partners

If you're a public company, your employee stockholders actually are your partners. This is the best kind of motivation. I encourage my key people to be heavily invested in Worldwide Entertainment and Sports because then they have a vested interest in the company's success. How much money they make off their shares is tied directly into the overall success of the company, which is tied into how hard they work. Employees who own stock know that if the company goes down, they go down, too. Talk about motivation!

If you're not a public company with shares to sell, you can still use the profits of the company to motivate your employees. Give your key people a financial interest in the company: maybe a yearly percentage of profits. Or if you're in sales, offer a higher commission when they go over a certain point. Or offer bonuses to employees who meet personal goals, or to everyone if the company meets a given goal. And look into an ESOP (employee stock ownership plan) as a form of profit-sharing.

Personal gain is a strong motivator. Offer your people some kind of financial incentive to concentrate and work hard. This may be money right out of your own pocket, but it always costs money to make money.

Give them the right tools

We all need the right tools to stay motivated. My recruiters, for example, need certain props to convince people that Worldwide Entertainment and Sports is a big-time, credible organization. To do this, they might need a limousine, a private plane, plenty of cash, or access to the best restaurants and clubs. It's my job to make sure they have everything they need to be effective in what they do. Of course, we're all working within a budget, and sometimes they'll fly economy class, stay in economy hotels, and eat in fast-food restaurants. But when first class is necessary to reach a business goal—first class it is.

In all businesses, there are certain tools that are necessary for people to have confidence in their ability to do their job. These motivating tools might be the latest (and functioning) computers, copy machines, up-to-date mailing lists, fax machines, cellular phones, company cars, or an entertainment budget. What is it in your business? Before you jump at an answer, ask the people you're working with what *they* think they need to do the job you expect them to do.

If you really believe your business will benefit from having motivated employees, then it's your job to give them what they need to do their job better than the employees who work for your competitors. You can't honestly expect a can-do attitude from an employee who has to run to the corner store to send or receive faxes. Or from people who have to take customers out to dinner, but can't afford a decent set of clothes. Give your employees what they need to feel pride in themselves and in their work. You'll see the results in improved attitude—and profits.

Give your employees the tools they need to show your customers and clients that your company is the best in the business.

Map out goals and rewards

Every business has goals that have to be met, but not every business lets the employees know what those goals are. That's a big mistake. We all need to know what we're trying to accomplish—beyond today's paycheck. I sit down with the key people in my organization and we set goals based on yearly statistics. In black and white, we can see how we have advanced each year and how many players we have to acquire in the coming year to reach the goals we set. We can see several years ahead how, step-by-step, we'll bring in millions if we all meet our goals. For all of us, that's the light at the end of the tunnel. We can see what we're working for.

To meet these goals, my people know I expect them to deliver. Every year the recruiters are supposed to come up with top draft choices or sign some star veterans who are unhappy with their agents. The marketing guys have to come up with big endorsement deals. And I have to have a few guys fighting for a championship every year. If we're all not meeting these expectations, then we're all out of business.

In every business, employees need goals and they need to know what they'll get if they meet those goals. Give your employees rewards that motivate, maybe a raise, a promotion, a bonus, an equity stake in the company, increased stock options, increased budget, another secretary, an assistant, something! Everybody needs to know that with results come rewards.

We all need to know where we're going and what we'll get when we get there. Give all your employees clear goals and incentives.

Keep talking

Communication is the lifeblood of a successful organization. Not only does it create loyalty as I mentioned earlier, it's also key to keeping people motivated. If you're interested in what your employees are doing and if you want to help them reach their goals, don't assume they know this—tell them. I schedule meetings just to talk about employee needs. I ask them directly: What props do you need to do your job? What money do you need to reduce financial headaches? What concerns do you have? I want to make sure all our cards are always on the table. They know I'm available 24 hours a day, seven days a week.

Communication is also important for keeping a team working together. I've got key people all over the country who need to know that they're not out there alone. We all meet once a month to share what's going on. Many times it turns out, for example, that the basketball guy is managing a player who's best friends with a top-pick football player—this helps the football recruiter do his job. Or the football guy may be managing a player who's best friends with a basketball player who's unhappy with his agent—he'll pass this news on at our meeting. Or maybe the marketing guy has an endorsement deal that he has to give out to somebody. At these meetings, we'll work out who gets it so nobody feels like things are happening behind closed doors. We always leave these meetings in a better position to do our jobs.

> *Everyone in the organization needs to feel like we're all on the same team (and the same page). The more we help each other, the better it is for everybody. We're in this together.*

Stand back

If you treat people like kids you can't trust, they'll act like kids you can't trust. That's why I don't think you can motivate people by looking over their shoulders every minute. Micromanaging steals initiative, creativity, and joy. It's degrading and counterproductive. Your employees need some freedom to find ways to meet their goals.

My people have a lot of freedom and leeway. They have to, because we're spread out all over the country without any direct supervision or ties to an office. I can't be involved in every draft choice in every sport who my people decide to go after. Sure it was obvious that my football recruiter, Joel Segal, would go after Tyrone Wheatley who was the most highly recruited guy out of Michigan ever and a projected first-round pick, but when he decided to go after Terrell Davis, a seventh-round pick out of Georgia, who knew he'd later become one of the hottest running backs in the NFL? I have to trust that my recruiters will make good decisions, and decisions that are good for the company. Most often, I'm not disappointed.

I'm not saying that I want my people to get out and fend for themselves completely. I'm always there if they need me. I'm glad to step in to open some doors or give my opinion if they ask for it. I like to manage by giving people whatever they need to do things their way, and then send them off to do it.

> *If you want the people who work for you to take personal responsibility for meeting their goals, give them the freedom they need to map out their own route to these goals.*

Manage the fear

There's nothing wrong with fear as a motivating force—if it is self-imposed. Fear of going bankrupt, of going hungry, of letting people down, of losing a big account to a competitor—circumstances like these are all motivating.

If you're in a business that's very competitive and stressful, you can use this self-imposed fear to motivate your employees. But be careful. Too much internal fear can freeze a person's ability to function. So keep everyone's focus on the positive and mix fear with high hopes. This will fill your staff with people who are motivated and determined.

It is how you handle fear that matters. When one of my boxers steps into the ring, you bet he feels fear (a guy will be throwing punches at his head!). But fear is the thing that keeps the boxer focused and intent—one lapse in attention and it's all over. That's the kind of fear that's positive. In my business, every day is like getting into the ring to dodge punches. The stakes are high and there are a billion people trying to make the big money, but there are only a handful of people who actually do it. If my staff isn't consistently at the top of their game, we'll be knocked out real fast. This thought fills all of us with a nagging fear. But on the other hand, we all know that if we work hard and work together, we'll be among the select few who *will* make millions in this business. The determination to stay on top and the fear of failing balance each other and get us positive results.

Solid teamwork also builds an internal fear that is very motivating. My guys are all very close with each other and with the athletes, so there's a personal fear of letting each other down. If the company failed because they didn't give 110 percent, there's no way any of them could look at themselves in the mirror. Do your employees love their work so much that they're afraid to let you and other employees down?

When you create a positive work environment with lots of support, you also create a fear of failure—that's a good motivator.

Motivating yourself

At the same time that I'm looking for ways to motivate my employees, I have to keep myself motivated, too. Mostly, my motivation comes from somewhere inside—I can see that the higher I climb, the hungrier I get. I know lots of people who accomplish their goals, feel satisfied, and spend more time playing golf. I can't do that. I've set my goals very high: to be the top entertainment/sports company in all fields. The closer I get to that goal, the more anxious I am to jump up another level.

These are the things that keep me motivated:

Successful people. I keep myself hungry by reading everything I can get my hands on about people who are absolutely tops in their fields. I figure I'm nothing until I get in that same position.

The unknown. I talk to people all day long who have great ideas for new and exciting things. I never know when I'm going to hear one that I think is great and want to run with. All the endless possibilities that are out there keep me motivated.

The unexplored. Being the first person to go public with a sports management company was a tremendous rush for me. I'm always on the lookout for opportunities to be innovative and pioneering. I love paving new paths.

Being on top. My business is in a very competitive market, and there are only a handful who can make it big. My determination to be one of that handful motivates me every morning.

Being busy. I always keep my plate full and look for new and interesting things to try. Like this book; it's something I've never done before and I'm having a great time with it. I'll never let myself be bored.

The spotlight. If I get my name out into the media and people start to look up to me as an expert, I've got to come through or lose face. That's very motivating. Tell everybody you're the best and watch how fast you get motivated to become the best.

My mentors. The people who have taught me and supported me are very special in my life. I can't let them down. I'll keep working at full steam to show them that their trust and support were not wasted.

Fear. It hasn't been easy to get to where I am. I always think back to when I first started and had nothing. I don't want to get careless or cocky and lose what I've worked so hard for.

Critical life lessons

- ✓ Not all employees are self-motivated.
- ✓ If you motivate with intimidation, you'll get quick results. But you'll also lose employee loyalty, which will hurt you in the end.
- ✓ The daily count of compliments should far outnumber complaints.
- ✓ Employees should feel personal ownership in the success or failure of the company.
- ✓ The boss who takes full credit for the success of the company is bound to have an organization full of resentful people.
- ✓ Employees who share the limelight are proud of their work.
- ✓ Financial incentives are great motivators.
- ✓ The right tools make any job easier and any employee more productive.
- ✓ Society is structured around rewards: school diplomas, Olympic medals, political appointments, etc. Employees, too, need rewards to strive for.
- ✓ A silent workplace kills employee motivation. Employees need an opportunity to talk about their concerns, their needs, and their triumphs.
- ✓ Micromanaging steals employees' sense of personal responsibility. To be internally motivated, we all need freedom to find our own work style.
- ✓ Fear of failure is a great motivator if it is balanced with high hopes and determination.
- ✓ A positive approach to mistakes and problems will bring everyone back up to peak performance much faster than a blaming, scolding approach.
- ✓ Self-motivation comes from identifying the things that make you want to get up in the morning and then having the freedom to go after them.

Nurture Loyalty

---

*I need to know that the people around me are loyal. If they're not,
they'll cheat, lie, and steal me right out of business. If they're not, I'd
wake up each morning worrying about being stabbed in the back at
every turn. If the people around me aren't loyal, I can't function.
That's why I put a lot of time and effort into building loyalty in my
clients, customers, investors, employees, and friends.*

Loyalty is important in all walks of life. It's the trait that gives
you the peace of mind you need to move forward through your life
without worrying all the time—without worrying that someone you
trust will turn against you, lie about you, be underhanded, or work
both sides of a deal. It's one of the most important traits you can build
in your personal and business associates and friends.

Client loyalty: It's more than just closing a deal

Athletes are my clients. My recruiters and I work hard to identify
the top prospects, evaluate their career potential, and decide who we'll
recruit. The loyalty factor plays a big part in the players we choose
because I have to judge right up front who is going to stay with us. It
takes an awful lot of time, money, and energy to bring an athlete into
Worldwide Entertainment and Sports. If I'm going to invest in an
athlete and bust my behind to build his career, I need to know that
he's not going to turn and run as soon as some other agent dangles an
incentive under his nose.

The key to getting this loyalty is something very basic: I have to
show them that I have their best interests at heart and that I would
never compromise or sacrifice anything in my dealings with them.

Roberts Rules!

You earn people's loyalty by putting their needs before your own.
This isn't idealistic rhetoric, it's a very practical fact.

Because we get many athletes when they're young, they look to us for guidance—but that doesn't mean we take over their lives. It's not in their best interest to keep them in the dark. They have to understand the financial side of their careers. They have to know where the money is going. They have to learn to take responsibility for what they do and what they say. We try to teach them and help them mature and grow in the business. We encourage them to make plans to do something when their playing days are over.

This really comes down to good communication. If I want their loyalty, I have to let the athletes know the state of affairs, let them in on the decision-making process, give them a say in everything that affects their career, help them understand everything that's going on. Showing an honest concern for their lives and their needs builds the loyalty I need. The same premise is true for any client in any business.

You won't get client loyalty by shielding them from the day-to-day business decisions. You have to bring your clients into the middle of things. They have to feel that they always know what's going on.

Your clients also need to know that you appreciate their business. You have to treat them like they are the most important people in the world. In the 1997 NBA draft, we had two of the top 23 players. My recruiters wanted to throw a party for them, not even knowing at that time how high on the list they would be drafted. The recruiters knew that a blow-out party would make the athletes feel special no matter where they were drafted. So down in Charlotte, N.C., where the draft was held, we put together a bunch of parties for our recruits: Bobby Jackson who went to the Denver Nuggets, and Derek Anderson who went to the Cleveland Cavaliers. (Both went on to play in the NBA Rookie All-Star Game in 1998.) We invited their friends, teammates, fans, and families. This little celebration cost me about $10,000 and, of course, people told me I was crazy. I admit, that is a lot of money to spend on guys you've already signed. And I can tell you there were no other agents down there putting out that kind of money for their athletes. But signing a player isn't the end goal. The real job is to build a relationship, a bond, right from the start that will keep the players loyal in the long run.

When the deal is signed, you're just beginning. That's the time to invest more time and money to build a loyal, long-term relationship.

What I was buying was loyalty. These lavish parties showed the athletes we care about them; it showed that we are proud of them; we have confidence in them. This was an investment in long-term relationships. From that point of view, $10,000 isn't such a high price.

You can't build client loyalty without taking a very personal interest in their lives right from the start. When I signed Ray Mercer, I moved him right into my house. When I started working with Shannon Briggs, I moved him into my house, too. This may be an extreme way of taking care of clients, but I had my reasons. I knew that when these guys made it big, the whole world was going to be luring them away from me. Everybody would tell them they could be making more money and getting better fights. It just goes with the territory. I create loyalty from day one.

You finish up how you start. If you want your clients to be loyal to you in the end, you have to treat them right in the beginning.

You have to prove to your clients that you care about their success. With Mercer and Briggs, I proved this by watching closely over their training. I made sure they got up to run at 5 a.m. I made sure they were eating right and not messing around with girls. That set them on the right course for their careers. These were young guys; if they weren't right under my nose, who knows what they would have been doing. In the four to five years my boxers lived with me, we built a bond of friendship. They saw firsthand how much I care for them and that I'm good at what I do. During those years, I earned a soft spot in their hearts; now they know the real deal when other people try to turn them against me.

This is key. You can't sign clients and then ignore them—they'll be gone before you know what happened.

You also have to make sure that you don't dump people as soon as their luck runs out. When people you've been close to and have supported are down, that's when you should be right by their side—at least half of them will come back. And when they do, they'll do anything for you to repay your having stood by them. This is a real loyalty builder. When people are up on top, everybody is by their side. But when they're down-and-out or still struggling to get to the top, they remember the people who stick by them.

Customer loyalty: It can't be taken for granted

Just like anybody else in business, I have customers—my customers are the fans. Their loyalty is absolutely necessary to the success of my business, because if fans don't buy the tickets and merchandise, my athletes don't need a manager or an agent. I can't assume that an athlete or a team will be so consistently great that the fans will always love them. You can't assume that your product or service is so great that your customers will automatically stay with you. You have to actively work to get customer loyalty—you want them to like you and your product so much that they'll stick around in good times—and bad.

If you think you can succeed in business without working hard to create customer loyalty, think again. Without customer loyalty, you have nothing.

The first thing I do to keep my fans loyal is to keep in touch with them—thousands of them! I figure if I constantly update people about my athletes, they'll start to feel like they're insiders, like somehow they have a vested interest in the athlete and his success. Through our mailing list, I'm constantly sending out information about the company: Who have we signed? What's the next event? The more people know about the athlete, the more likely they are to root for him and buy tickets to see him—and want to see more. I create a following of people who feel like they're part of the organization. That's where the loyalty factor comes in, big time.

Nobody has the fan loyalty I have. But nobody else has a sales force that actually telephones fans and tells them when there's an event and where the party afterwards will be. My fans know that if I'm involved, every sporting event is a good time. Fans don't only want to watch sports, they want to have fun. I can't control what happens at the team sports, but when I promote my own boxing matches, I make sure the fans feel like they've gotten their money's worth. For the guys, I always invite a lot of pretty girls. And the girls love to come because they know there'll be a lot of eligible guys around. I bring in national TV for the effects of lights, cameras, and action. I throw a party afterward. Just because fans buy tickets doesn't mean they're loyal. I have to make sure they have fun and that they feel special—then they'll become loyal.

*Customer loyalty doesn't come cheap—but neither does success.
Any investment in loyalty pays impressive dividends.*

It's especially great to have fan loyalty in an instance like the time Shannon Briggs fought George Foreman in 1997. Briggs won the fight, but it was a controversial decision, and the place went wild. While the Foreman fans were booing and throwing things, it was great to hear the Briggs fans cheering, clapping, hooting, stomping, and yelling. They wrote us letters saying they were proud of Briggs and they knew he won the fight legitimately. They stuck by us. This meant a lot to Shannon, and it also meant a lot to me and to the stability of my business.

*The value of loyalty can't be fully appreciated until things go bad.
That's when it becomes a priceless asset.*

Even in our team sports, we try to build fan loyalty for the sake of our players. One of our football players, Antonio Freeman of the Green Bay Packers, for example, has some of the most loyal fans in the world. These people are unbelievable. Freeman would have been named MVP of the 1998 Super Bowl if the Packers had won. Still, the fans supported him. After the loss, 35,000 fans showed up at the stadium for a pep rally! This kind of support gives the athletes lots of mental strength to keep going and keep reaching for the top. Obviously, the harder they try, the better for their careers and the better for me.

This kind of loyalty can't be taken for granted; it has to be rewarded. We work hard to make sure our fans know they're special— that's why we have a marketing department (most sports agencies don't). We have people who call all over the local area and get our guys appearances at places like car dealerships, malls, and charity events so the fans can see them and talk to them. If our fans call us and say they're supporting a charity and having an auction, we'll always send over autographed gloves, footballs, basketballs. We hand out pictures of our guys at the stadiums and arenas so everybody can have them. We make sure our big athletes respond to their fan mail. For the fans in Wisconsin, we got Antonio Freeman his own TV show so they can see him and call in and talk with him. This is our way of thanking our customers for their loyalty. I can't expect them to stick around in the tough times unless I can convince them that their support is valued and appreciated.

Loyalty happens when you go out of your way to show people you appreciate what they do for you.

The financial value of this kind of customer loyalty cannot be calculated. You know that when your customers are loyal and create a steady demand for your product or service, business is strong. You can negotiate better contracts. You can charge higher prices. You can even put a price tag on the value of name recognition. People like Antonio Freeman and our Giants running back Tyrone Wheatley get endorsement contracts because their names mean a lot to the fans. In any business, the more loyalty you have, the more business you'll do, the more people will buy your stock, and the more people will tell others about your company. Loyalty creates a domino effect that's great for business.

Loyalty automatically improves the bottom line.

Investor loyalty: It's more than money

I need investor loyalty and I spend a lot of time and effort to get it. When I discussed networking in Rule #4, I mentioned that my investors are on top of my priority list. I have several important investors who I want to personally stay in touch with to show my appreciation and to gain their loyalty. I always call these people to give updates on what's going on. I go to dinner with them every few weeks. Again, this is all about communication. I can't expect an investor to stay loyal if I don't stay in touch.

You can't expect investor loyalty if you take a person's money and run with it without looking back.

You should also try to do things that bring your investors right into the middle of the action. They own a piece of the business—they should be involved. In my business, I can sit my investors down in the front row at a sporting event. I can take them into the locker room. I can take them out to dinner with players. I can get them player autographs and pictures. At games they have a right to feel, "Hey, that's my guy playing down there." It's my job to make sure they feel like they own a piece of something very important.

Your investors own a piece of your business. What can you do to bring them into the middle of things? What do you have to offer that can make an investor proud? Does your company win awards? Does it get any publicity? Do you get press coverage for community involvement? Do you have company parties where you can invite your investors as VIP guests and publicly acknowledge their support? You have to do something to build pride of ownership in your investors.

Sure, my investors feel proud when I do things like give them great seats to a major sporting event, but it's not the favor alone that builds their loyalty—it's the fact that I always come through with what I say. If I say they're going to get third-row seats, they don't get fourth row. If I say an athlete is coming to dinner with us next Tuesday night, the athlete will be at dinner with us next Tuesday night. If I tell an investor to bring his or her best client to a game and I'll get them into the locker room after the game, they're going to get into the locker room. Other people will make promises like this, but not follow through. Their promises are big and so are their excuses: "Oh, well, this is a bad time," or "Something came up at the last minute to change the plans." I won't promise anybody anything unless I can come through. This says a lot about the way I do business with an investor's money in general. Bottom line: I do what I say I'm going to do. This is a tried and true way to earn loyalty.

Don't ever make a promise you can't keep. It destroys loyalty.

Now that Worldwide Entertainment and Sports is a public company, I have many investors I don't know personally, but whose loyalty I still want to earn. We know who our stockholders are and we keep in touch. Just like our other customers, we send them fliers and mailers; we put many of them on my fax list so they get any news about the company right away. We make announcements on the Dow Jones when anything significant happens. Our investors' relations department takes care of letting our stockholders know what's going on. Our ticket department will actually call our investors personally to tell them about upcoming events and offer them first-choice tickets. Our goal is to turn some of these stockholders into major investors by doing the fundamental things that are guaranteed to build loyalty.

Investors take a leap of faith when they hand over their money. It's important to repay that faith by giving them your time, your attention, and your appreciation. This is a very concrete way of saying thank you. Remember, appreciation and loyalty go hand in hand.

Keep in touch with your investors. Let them know exactly how their money is being spent and how their support is helping your business.

Employee loyalty: It's absolutely vital

People in business are always complaining about lack of loyalty from their employees. They gripe that employees jump from one company to another always looking for a better offer and not caring who they leave behind. But I see the problem differently. Employees don't show up at a new job already full of loyalty. They arrive completely neutral and will hold on to their allegiances until they find out if loyalty has something to offer to them. Employee loyalty has to be built and nurtured by the employer.

I work hard at building employee loyalty for a lot of reasons—most of them, I admit, are selfish ones. For starters, it costs me money every time an employee leaves. An incredible amount of effort, time, and company resources are required to identify and hire a good employee. Once the person is on board, he or she still has to get used to the job and "get up to speed" in the position. During this training time, reduced productivity and lost sales opportunities or customers are costly.

To keep any business running smoothly, it's critical to keep high-performing employees. It's my job to create the loyalty that will keep them in my company. I have to always be aware that there are people out there trying to steal away my best people. (Believe me, I know—so many of my people are always being lured to other agencies!) So I have to make sure that I constantly give my employees good reasons to stay with me. I have to make them feel secure and supported. They need to know that their work is recognized and appreciated.

If you want your employees to be loyal right from the start, the right hand has to know what the left hand is doing. It keeps the company running smoothly and it keeps the employees from stepping all over each other. It would be easy for my college recruiters to start competing with each other for the same athletes. But this makes the whole company look bad, and it also makes the recruiters feel like they're out there on their own with no support. To prevent this, we have meetings; we have phone conferences; we have lots of personal get-togethers so that everyone knows we're all on the same team working toward the same goal.

> *If your organization breaks into splintered groups who work to meet their own goals, you can expect expensive mistakes and costly turnovers.*

In my business, where I spend so much time with big-name athletes and my key employees are jetting all over the country and getting their names in the news, it would be easy to overlook my home-base employees. But I need their loyalty, too. One way I try to nurture that is by making sure they don't feel left out of this exciting industry. Everybody from my limo driver to my secretaries should feel like they are a part of this company. I want them at the boxing matches and basketball games, right in the company seats where they're treated special—because they are special.

People who feel special and valued will do anything for you. This is most evident in the homeless guys who help out at my New York nightclub, the China Club. They were down on their luck, so I gave them work. They sell flowers, they get cars and cabs for the patrons, they run the street, and I treat them with respect. I can leave my most important guests in their hands while they wait for limos to arrive and I know they'll be treated like gold, because these guys would run through fire for me—they tell me that all the time. All it takes is giving people what they need, treating them kindly, and taking the time to chat about nothing special every once in a while.

Your employees have to believe that you genuinely care for them. They need to feel needed and respected. Obviously, this takes a personal touch and can't be handled through office memos. My employees have no doubt that I care about them. If they call me and ask for something, they know that if it's possible, I'll get it. They know I won't make a promise and then drop out of sight. The fastest way to lose employees is to be all talk and no action. If you promise an employee a vacation, a bonus, or a valued account, make sure you can deliver.

Another loyalty booster comes from being willing to give employees a little extra once in a while. We're working off a nice big pie, I'll share it with everyone—and try to give more than expected. On special birthdays, for instance, I'll tell them to use the company limo and take their family out for a nice dinner on me. I'm always catering to our athletes; it's important to cater to my top employees, too. I think little things like this go a long way.

You can also create loyalty by helping your employees in their personal lives. I've given loans right out of my pocket to my employees. In fact, when the president of our basketball division wanted to move into a house, I handed him a bonus to cover the down payment. Talk to your employees. Find out what's going on with their families and their children. Find out how you can help them with personal needs. Encourage them to tell you when they have a problem. My employees know I'll do anything for them. And I know they'll do anything for me.

There's no denying that employee turnover is expensive. So save yourself some money by nurturing employee loyalty—give them attention, respect, and a helping hand when necessary.

Day-to-day loyalty

Every day of your life, you should do something to ensure that you are surrounded by loyal people. They are the foundation of your success.

Let's be honest: When push comes to shove, you can count on loyalty that's rooted in personal gain over loyalty based on friendship. This is the real world we live in. You may have a few people in your life you can count on no matter what happens. But what about the rest? Make it your business to give them a reason to stay loyal.

Critical life lessons

- ✓ If you want client loyalty, make sure you put their needs before your own.

- ✓ Earn people's trust by bringing them into the middle of things.

- ✓ Treat the people you deal with like they're the most important people in the world, and they'll follow you anywhere.

- ✓ Loyalty and appreciation go hand in hand.

- ✓ The fastest way to lose someone's loyalty is to lose contact.

- ✓ Loyalty doesn't happen because you're a nice person; it happens because you make a conscious effort to earn it.

- ✓ Loyalty can be expensive, but lack of loyalty can bankrupt you.

- ✓ Loyalty can be put on or faked. Gauge true loyalty by how fiercely people stick by you in hard times.

- ✓ Time, attention, and appreciation are proven loyalty builders.

- ✓ Being stingy with your employees saves you pennies and costs you dollars.

- ✓ If you're having a problem with employee turnover, you're not doing enough to earn employee loyalty.

- ✓ Make it a priority to surround yourself with loyal people.

Pay Attention

*Every very successful person can name the project that made the
difference in his or her life—the make-it-or-break-it deal. When
you're getting into that kind of project, you've got to learn how to pay
attention. I mean full, total focus. That's all you do. That's all you
think about. That's your only goal.*

I'm a single guy and my life style ever since I was 19 has been to
work hard, then go out and have fun until three or four in the morning. I go to restaurants and clubs and meet with people when they're
relaxed and having a good time. I enjoy it, and it's good for business.
But when I decided to take Worldwide Entertainment and Sports
public, I had to change this style of living. It didn't take me long to
figure out that maybe the reason no other sports agency was going
public was because it's a very difficult thing to do and it requires an
incredible amount of commitment and focus.

For the entire year before the deal went through, I woke up at
seven in the morning and went to bed at nine at night. I completely
stopped socializing with my friends. I didn't go out at night at all—
well, maybe once in a while, but it really was a total life-style change.
There was just so much that had to get done, I couldn't scatter my
energy in different directions. I had to network and make connections
with the people who believed in me and could help me. I was spending days and days with lawyers, accountants, investment bankers,
advisors, investors, and brokers. I had to roll the limited partnership
with investors who had invested in the boxers into common stock and
get them all to sign off on it. I had to sell the whole idea to brokerage firms. I had to deal with the SEC and NASDAQ through regis-
trations. In the best of circumstances, this process can be overwhelming. But remember, I was also facing the challenge of trying to change

the course of the business plans right in the middle of negotiations (after Shannon lost the big fight that was the glue of the deal). Of course at the same time I still had a company to run and was busy taking care of business.

To get all this done, I literally disappeared from the social scene for a year. I didn't like it, but I knew this deal was important—it would change my life. When you have stakes like that, you have to be willing to sacrifice in order to focus.

Day and night, eat, sleep, and breathe your goal. If you aren't willing to give this venture all your attention, time, and energy, it probably won't happen.

Obstacles to focusing

Staying focused is hard enough in the best of circumstances. Throw in a collection of obstacles and the odds against success grow even higher. In the hope that forewarned is forearmed, take a look at a few of the obstacles you can expect to run into and be ready for them.

Other business distractions

You have to prioritize what's most important when you have a big project in front of you. Maybe you're going public, or building a major factory overseas, or building a building, or whatever. You know what has to be done, but are you able or willing to cut out other things in your life to focus on this project? Too many major projects going on at the same time will sabotage your efforts. You can't do it all. When you're going into a venture that will make or break you, you can think of it like going to war. You have to put all your best people, your best strategies, your best of everything in one place. You can't be at war all over the map and expect to win anything. You have to identify the opportunity that will make the difference in your life and go after it with both barrels with *nothing* on the side distracting you.

When I decided to expand my sports management to include football and basketball, I knew I couldn't possibly run everything. I couldn't recruit football and basketball players, do marketing and public relations, manage fighters, handle stockbrokers, investment bankers, and investors, run the business, and raise money all at the same time. Some people try, but they don't do it successfully. Part of focusing on what's important is knowing when and how to delegate to other people so you're not torn in different directions. I've hired top-quality people to look after the football, basketball, and marketing ends of the business. I give them all the weapons they need to do their job better than anybody out there. Their job is to give these areas their full and total attention. While they're focusing on the individual parts of the whole, I can keep my end goal in sight while avoiding the obstacle of other business distractions.

There's such a slight difference between successful and unsuccessful people. This is most obvious among people with equal talent and intellect. Why does one make it and not the other? It's all mental. The successful ones stay mentally disciplined and focused.

Feeling overwhelmed

Many major projects seem to loom in the unattainable distance. There's so much to get done, so many steps, so much to do. Looking at all the many pieces of the big picture stops some people dead in their tracks. They see a 5,000-piece jigsaw puzzle with its pieces scattered all over the floor. They don't even know where to begin to put it together, so they sweep it back into the box and forget about it. Other people will sit right down in the middle of the mess and start organizing. They know how to put like parts together and map out a plan of attack, one piece at a time. This is what success-driven people have to be willing to do. Taking one small step forward every day will eventually bring you to the end of even the most outrageously difficult project.

My big-picture goal has been to be the biggest all-sports management company in the country. That's a tall order that's seemingly impossible. How can one company be the best in boxing and at the same time the best in football? And in basketball? And in race-car driving? And in marketing? And in the stock market? That all seems too overwhelming. But I know I'm going to do it. And I'll do it by setting doable goals in every division every year. As I reach each one, I'll be another step closer to reaching the big goal.

Last year, we were one of the top two agents involved in the basketball draft. (In the NBA draft, if you don't get players in the top 30 to 35 picks, you're out of business.) My goal is to do the same thing again this year. In football, I need to again pick a star or two. There are five billion people going after these guys—I have to be one of the ones who signs them. I'll focus on doing whatever needs to get done to make sure I meet these goals. They're the ones that are going to help me reach my long-range goal.

If you're not meeting your monthly goals, you're taking small steps in the wrong direction. You'll never reach your long-term goal unless you change direction and get back on track.

Impatience

Big gains don't come quickly. Be patient with yourself and give yourself the time you need to be successful—realistically. I'd love to be the biggest sports management company in the country at the end of this year, but that's unrealistic. We're on a three- to five-year plan that I know is doable—but it's going to take discipline to stay focused that long.

Look down the road. How long do you think it should take to reach your big-picture goal? Don't rush yourself; that's too frustrating and throws more obstacles in your path. Be reasonable and patient. Then set a date, write it down, and keep it in a place where you can see it often. This is where you're headed.

Being focused is a long-term discipline because nothing great happens overnight. Some people will get frustrated and give up—of course that completely blows their chances of making it to the top.

Complacency

Sometimes when the ball gets rolling and things seem to be falling into place, people lose their focus and everything falls apart. I've seen guys work so hard and get so close and then get careless and lose it all. That's what Donald Trump says happened to him when he almost went bankrupt. He says he lost his focus. He started thinking it was too easy and he took his eye off the eight ball. It happens all the time, even to the best of them.

Losing the edge because of complacency happens in every profession in the world, but it's especially obvious in sports. So many guys get right to the verge of making big money, then they start believing all the great things the press and their fans say about them. They get cocky and lazy and they don't train as hard. Many start hanging out with the wrong people. This kills their focus and they fall apart. I look at guys like Mike Tyson, or baseball's Ruben Sierra, or basketball's Ralph Sampson. It looks to me like they lost their focus. They stopped doing the things that got them to that high point in the first place.

When you're on the verge of making it big, things won't stay status quo—you're either going to make it or you're going to lose focus and fall.

As you get closer to your goals, don't loosen up on the reins of determination—tighten up. Remember what it took for you to get that far and respect the effort by staying on track. When I could see that my plan to go public was really going to happen, I didn't celebrate by going out with my friends. I decided to work even harder to make sure nothing would go wrong, that I hadn't overlooked anything, that everybody had what they needed. Getting closer made me hungrier and encouraged me to stay focused.

Too many obligations

Many ambitious people are very involved in life. They are members of service groups. They coach youth sports teams. They're on the board of their temple or church. They're involved with foundations and charities. This is all very fulfilling and important work. But when you need to focus, these things are too much of a drain on your time and energy.

Look at your life and the commitments you've made. Which ones can you put aside for a while? Which ones can you cut out completely? Which ones give to rather than take from your store of strength and energy? Answering these questions will help you organize your plan for reaching your goal.

> *Unfortunately, you can't do it all—especially when your future is on the line. If you're married and have kids, well of course you want to be available to them, but everything else that pulls your attention away from your work has to go until you reach your goal.*

Financial worries

If you're waking up each morning wondering how you're going to pay the mortgage or your kid's tuition, you're not in a position to focus on a life-changing project. You have to make sure that you have nothing else to think about except how to reach your goals. Before you begin, you should sit down and go over a monthly budget. Map out exactly what income you need so you can focus on your goals without worrying about paying the bills. If the amount is too much to leave you worry-free, you have to downgrade.

Downgrading means you move to a smaller place, you get an older car, you stop going to the best restaurants, you give up your season tickets. These moves shouldn't discourage you—they should motivate you! Now you have a personal reason to focus on your goal and work hard to reach it. When I was 22 and achieved a level of financial success, I bought a huge home for myself in a neighborhood I always dreamed of living in. If I later found that the cost of maintaining that house was distracting me from my work, I would have had no problem selling it. I would have rented a cheaper apartment and saved a couple thousand dollars a month. Doing that would have given me more cash flow and it would have also motivated me. I would wake up every morning determined to do whatever I could to buy another great house. (Actually, I'd probably set my sights on an even bigger house so I'd know that my sacrifice would put me in a better position than where I started.)

Whatever you have to do to cut your bills is worth it if it frees you from financial worries that would distract you from your goal. It takes too much energy to spend half your day figuring out how to rob Peter to pay Paul. You can't focus like that. Before you jump with both feet into a big deal, look over your finances. Maybe you'll have to put off the project, maybe you can cut back on expenses or downgrade your life style, or maybe you can get a $100,000 loan to cover your expenses for the time you'll be tied up. Do whatever you have to do to free yourself of financial worries.

Friends and family

The people who love you can be the biggest obstacles. They'll say, "Come on, you're getting obsessed with this project. Let's go out. Let's forget about work for a while. Let's go on vacation." They don't understand your position and your decision to focus. Let me warn you now: For lots of reasons, people will try to sway your determination to stay focused. Be ready for them.

When boxer Shannon Briggs went on Howard Stern's radio show a few days before he fought for the World Heavyweight Championship against Lennox Lewis, Howard got on Shannon about his girlfriend, saying that they broke up because Shannon must have been cheating. Shannon set him straight and explained that when you're trying to focus on something this important, you don't have time to give other people what they need. He had no time or energy for his personal life.

Rejection

When you're reaching for your goal, there are going to be lots of people who say no: "No, you can't have this loan." "No, you can't have this building site." "No, you can't sell me that plan." People will hang up on you. Fifty people in a row will tell you to get lost. You may get only one yes out of a hundred people you talk to. This kind of rejection breaks the focus of all but the strongest. You've got to be persistent and keep going and going and going.

Many years ago when the cellular phone was introduced, I became a freelance salesperson. My job was to get people to contact the company for information, which wasn't easy because nobody had ever even heard of car phones, and because they were expensive. So I took the phone that I was given as a demo and I drove to the homes and offices of everybody I knew and showed them the phone. I asked each person to help me find out who would be interested in buying one. Then I would call everybody I knew every day and ask for some names. Of course, they'd start out saying, "I don't know anybody." After a few days, they'd say, "Here, try these two people." After a week of calling, they'd say, "If I give you 10 names, will you leave me alone?" After two or three weeks of daily phone calls, they'd give me their closest friends, enemies, colleagues, neighbors, anybody just to get me to stop calling. (My friend and attorney, Peter Ziering, still kids me about calling him every day without fail for 21 days.) I may have been a pain in the butt, but I didn't let rejection stop me, and eventually I got what I needed (and most of these people are still my friends).

---

*Always remember that the more people who say no to you, the closer you are to finding that one who will say yes. When I wanted to take my company public, I contacted more than **200** investment brokers looking for somebody to say yes. It only takes one.*

Jealousy

Believe it or not, not everyone will wish you well in your venture. There are always going to be people who hope you fall flat on your face, and they are not necessarily just your enemies. People in your own company may see you as a threat. It's tough to stay focused when you're being undermined by people who tell your clients, "Hey, you don't want to do business with him; he'll steal from you." It's tough to stay on track when your "advisers" say, "The odds are a hundred to one on that; don't even try." There are lots of people out there who don't want to see you succeed, but that shouldn't break your focus.

My world is full of jealous people who'd love to see me go bust. When Shannon Briggs won a controversial fight against George Foreman, lots of people started spreading lies that I had bought off the judges. (I didn't even know those judges!) But with this little bit of smoke, lots of people decided to start a fire. My competitors in boxing who are dying to bring me down leaked all kinds of lies to the press. It was open season for everyone who wanted to knock me down.

If you let them, these put-downs can get you off track. You can't stay focused if you spend too much mental and emotional energy trying to disprove the lies of jealous people. If you let them take your attention away from your goal, they've won.

The closer you get to reaching that goal, the more you're going to be the victim of rumors and lies. Don't let it distract you. Take the attention as a compliment and keep your eye on the target.

Personal problems

Personal problems can kill your concentration. Maybe you've been in a fight with someone, or you've lost an account, or your car got smashed in an accident. Whatever it is, it's interfering with your day's work. You've got to learn to block that out and focus. This will set you up to do some positive things that will neutralize the bad. If you sit around all day moaning about the bad, nothing good will happen. Any time you're faced with a negative, you've got to block it out and do something positive to regain the balance.

Losers dwell on problems. Winners block the problems out and do something positive to regain the advantage.

The things that keep you focused

Staying focused isn't easy. There are just so many things that can break your concentration and get you off track. To counter these negative influences, think about the things that encourage you to focus. There are lots of things that help me to stay focused. Try these.

Believe in what you're doing

There are hundreds of thousands of people out there working hard every day at something they hate. No matter how hard they work, they will never be the best. How can you stay really focused on something that doesn't completely consume you with enthusiasm? If you're going to go into a venture that you believe will be life-changing, make sure it's something that will jump-start you out of bed every morning. Having a passion for your work is a great way to get focused.

You need an air-tight package of belief to hold on to the focus that leads to success.

Celebrate reaching small goals

You should feel motivated to remain focused every time you reach one of the small goals that will lead you to your major long-term goal. Every time I sign another athlete, I say to myself, "God, this is working!" When I bring in a million bucks with a new investor, I say, "Hey, people are believing in me. This is good!" Every time WWES stock goes up a point, I feel more determined to make this work. Every small accomplishment is motivating. It keeps me on track and very focused.

Take time to celebrate small accomplishments. Sometimes people get so caught up in the big picture, they miss the pat on the back that's offered along the way. Every single time you take a step closer to your goal, stop and congratulate yourself. Your ego and your soul need to know that you're on the right course and all is well with the world.

Each time you attain a small goal, celebrate. That's your motivation to keep reaching for the top. Every little piece of positive reinforcement is the glue that keeps you on track.

Have a willingness to sacrifice

Sacrifice is not an appealing concept. We all work hard to reach the top so that we won't have to sacrifice the comforts of life. But ironically, I think a willingness to sacrifice is key to being successful.

If you're not willing to give up anything now for rewards later, forget it—you'll never make it.

My athletes know better than anybody how important personal sacrifice is. I won't sign an athlete unless he's the type of guy who is willing to sacrifice so he can stay focused. I want to work with guys who are willing to get up in the morning and go running, go to the gym, work with the strength coach, eat right. I want guys who are the first to report to training camp and the last to leave—the ones who train and practice all year round even when they become "superstars." I want the ones who are so focused, they're not messing around with drugs and all-night orgies. If I come across somebody who doesn't have this kind of focus, I don't want anything to do with him because he can't become a champion. I think this is true in any business.

To focus means to give all your energy and attention to one thing. This isn't easily done, especially in a world that is so full of distractions that it's hard to pay attention to anything for more than a minute and a half. But when you're ready to bet the farm, you'd also better be ready to focus.

Critical life lessons

✓ The ability to focus separates the successful from the unsuccessful.

✓ The most impossible feat is made up of very possible small accomplishments.

✓ Teach yourself patience—it will be good company during the long haul to success.

✓ There's nothing like the smell of success to make some people get lazy and complacent.

✓ Wipe out financial worries before you even think about focusing on a life-changing goal.

✓ Family and friends who love you dearly will be the first to tell you to give it up.

✓ If the rumors of jealous people can distract you from your goal, you don't have what it takes to play in the big leagues.

✓ When you believe in what you're doing with all your heart and soul, there isn't a force on Earth that can stop you.

✓ Never miss an opportunity to pat yourself on the back.

✓ Only if you're willing to sacrifice it all will you be in a position to have it all.

Advertise

I have a great company that does a lot of terrific things for our athletes. But I know that hard work and sound results alone aren't enough to make it really big. People have to know what we do; they have to recognize our name and connect it with prestige and success. That rarely happens by itself. I have to make sure that I get our name out to the public over and over again.

If you know you have a great product or service, you can't be afraid to shout about it. Be proud, be loud. Let everybody know you exist by advertising like crazy.

Get it in writing: Newspapers, magazines, books

Don't listen to people who say that nobody reads anymore. Sure, we get a lot of information from TV and computers, but newspapers, magazines, and books are still an essential route for getting your name out to the public.

Syndicated columnists are my first target in the print media. They write one story about you and it's all over the country. To me, that's better than a headline in one city paper any day. I try to get personally involved with columnists who have major circulation and who show they are open to giving my athletes some press. I call them up to talk. I put them on my fax list. I find out what their favorite charities are and I get involved in the ones that I want to support, too. I find out what teams they like and send them memorabilia. I give them news scoops for their region and keep them up-to-date all the time. I know these guys are worth my time and I make sure I give it to them.

Getting good press is great, but when it finally happens, don't sit around gloating over the story and let the opportunity to get the most out of it pass you by. When I get good coverage in one news region, I get a lot of mileage out of it. If the story runs in New York, I copy it and send it to papers in Dallas or Los Angeles and try to get the story to run again and again. Every piece of publicity has the potential to be recycled for more publicity.

Sometimes a news story runs because of a major business or sporting event, but usually I can't wait for my company or athletes to do something newsworthy to get press coverage—I make sure we generate our own press releases. When Ray Mercer got robbed in a fight against Lennox Lewis a couple of years ago, for example, Lewis wouldn't agree to a rematch. I couldn't get him to even talk to me. Then I woke up one morning with this great idea: I wrote a press release offering Lewis $20 million to fight Mercer. I added a twist by saying that if Mercer won, he would donate half of his winnings to the charity Project Pride in Newark, N.J. I sent it out over the Associated Press lines (which anyone can do if willing to pay the fee) and I made something happen. The offer made headlines all over the country. I put Lewis on the defensive and made him respond. (Time has shown that Lewis is no slouch. Just this year he pulled a page from my book by going to the press to publicly offer Evander Holyfield $20 million to fight him. This got him great headlines. He's learning!)

You have to be able to generate your own press coverage. If you sit around waiting for reporters to hear about you and your accomplishments, you'll die waiting. You've got to go on the offensive and contact them, let them know what you're doing. Build up enthusiasm for your work. Give them a unique or innovative hook they can grab onto to write something their readers will want to know about.

Get it together: Press book

Once the good stories have been printed (and reprinted if I'm lucky), that's still not the end of their value as a tool for exposure. We gather together all the best articles and put them into a press book. Then every three or four months, we update the book and keep about 30 of the latest and best pieces in there. These press books are regularly sent to investors and stockbrokers, our athletes, and future recruits so they always know we're still hot. (Once in a while, I'll even get a journalist to read it.) It looks very impressive when you can hand someone a bound packet of exciting articles.

Use any print exposure to get more exposure by sending it to all the right people: investors, brokers, clients, writers, and anyone you think is in a position to help you or to use your product or service.

Lights, camera, action: Videotapes

I make sure all of our accomplishments are on videotape because I think highlight tapes are an invaluable promotional tool. If something special is happening with the company, or with an athlete, or with me, or if I make a speech, or have a big party, or organize an event, we record it and put the best stuff on a highlight tape. Right now, I have a tape that focuses on the company, with interviews with my partners who head up the basketball, football, and marketing divisions. I have another showing the highlights of Shannon's career. And I have a tape that shows the best of my athletes in football, basketball, and boxing. This is a very visual world in which we live—almost everyone would rather see progress in action than read about it.

Making the tapes is an important step, but knowing exactly what to do with them is crucial. They do you no good if you get stingy and give them out only to top clients. You have to saturate the market with your tapes in order to reach your customers, clients, investors, and anybody who might be interested in supporting you.

I also send tapes of our athletes to the top news columnists, radio broadcasters, and sportscasters around the country. Then I make sure that someone from marketing follows up the mailing with phone calls. You have to push: "Did you get the tape? Isn't it great? There's a real story here." This step is very important. Everyone is busy and needs a reason to take the time to look at your tape. Your follow-up call (and the next call, and the calls after that) gives people that reason.

Sometimes we'll send out 1,000 to 2,000 tapes. Believe me, I know this is costly (we've spent as much as $10,000 on mailings), and then there's the cost of hiring competent people to make the follow-up phone calls. But I can't make money with a publicly traded company if people have never heard of us. Name recognition is priceless.

Every market has prime media targets—you have to find out who they are and let them know what you're doing—at any cost.

In addition to costing me money, videotapes also make me money. We send them to our investors to keep them involved in the athletes' progress. People are more likely to invest heavily if they feel like they're insiders who have some personal link to the athletes. Live-action tapes give this feeling. These tapes also help investors encourage their friends to invest, too. It's easy to say to a friend, "You've got to take a look at this tape. I think this company is really going places." But it's unlikely that too many people will take the time to explain to their friends why they've invested in our company. It's also better for me—the tape says exactly what I want potential investors to hear.

Of course, you have to be realistic about using videotapes to advertise. Not everybody is going to take your tape and play it— that's life. Some people are distracted with other things, some are busy, some are jealous. Whatever the reason, you're not going to wow everybody. So keep track of the people who, based on your follow-up calls, are at least willing to give your tapes a try, and put these people on your priority mailing list.

You have to identify who is willing to look at a videotaped promotion and who is not. This saves you money and helps you zero in on a receptive audience.

---

15 seconds of fame: TV

Television offers a variety of promotion opportunities—use all of them. When you're staging an event, such as a grand opening or a company-based charity benefit or community program, always invite TV reporters. Too many people think, "Oh, nobody would ever put a story about me or my company on TV." But with that kind of negative thinking, you have no chance at all. At least give it a try. And when the TV producer ignores you, try again and again, and then try different stations—especially the cable channels. There are actually stations out there looking for something local and upbeat to put on the air. Get to know your local station managers and reporters. Send them your highlight tapes, follow up with phone calls, and encourage them to cover your story.

Getting on TV is probably easier for me and my clients than for people in other businesses because big-name athletes draw viewers. But even still, there's competition for airtime, so I make sure that when I get it, I use it to my advantage. All the talk shows want to feature my big-name athletes, but very often I will agree to let a "name" athlete go on the show only if the producer allows him to bring along a lesser-known athlete who needs the exposure. Really big-name athletes don't need to spend too much of their time doing TV shows, but their popularity paves the way for the up-and-coming guys.

Once your product is known and sought after, don't stop promoting. Use the popularity of your product or service to promote some other aspect of your business.

Another thing I've learned about using TV to my advantage is to never shy away from live TV—the chance that something wild will happen (bringing even more coverage) is just too tempting to pass up. One time, for example, boxer Shannon Briggs got into a fight with Mitch "Blood" Green on *Sports Extra* (a popular Sunday night sports show on the Fox network). This was picked up on a highlight tape and shown all over the world. I didn't want the fight to happen, but it did and it ended up getting us more coverage than we could have dreamed of. There was another time when I was talking on live TV about the Riddick Bowe vs. Mercer fight. Bowe's manager, Rock Newman, kept interrupting me. So when he talked, I interrupted him. All of a sudden, Newman and four of his guys started pushing me around. That film showed for weeks all over the country. Then it was used in the opening montage on *USA Tuesday Night at the Fights* (USA cable TV) for a long time afterwards. Rock Newman and I both realized later that that incident gave both of us great exposure. We've worked together lots of times since then and have become good friends who agree: Don't ever turn down live TV—you can't buy the kind of publicity the unexpected can bring.

Mix it up: Think creatively

Lots of people lose great opportunities to get publicity because they think too narrowly. Then there are others who think creatively and make it work. Recently, I heard a great radio interview with Michael Drosnin, the guy who wrote the book *The Bible Code*. This is a pretty academic book that's been picked up for a documentary by PBS and is talked about in scholarly circles. But Drosnin was pitching it on New York's Z100 FM radio's "The Morning Zoo" right before a repeat performance of song parodies. Between crude and lewd commentaries, the DJ was telling listeners to get out and buy this book—now! It was a great piece of marketing.

I've always known that just because I'm in the sports business doesn't mean I have to focus only on sports media. When we want to make an athlete a household name, we reach past the sports pages. We get the athlete appearances on music media, we go on shock-jock radio, we get pieces in women's magazines like *Vogue*. You've got to think out of the box if you want to stand out from the crowd.

It's also good to work publicity from more than one angle. Yes, I'm involved with sports and I want coverage from sports writers, but I'm also a businessman and I go after press in business publications. To do this successfully, reporters need to know me. That's why I'll often invite big-name media people to dinner along with my investors, brokers, and recruiters. This shows the reporters another side of the business. I want them to get to know me as a person and get to know my company and the people who believe in and support me. When this happens, I get positive press in both business and sports arenas.

Hear ye! Hear ye!: Press conferences

When you want to draw media attention to your company, or your service, or whatever, call a press conference. Why not? When I want personal media attention, I set up a press conference and hope for the best. Sometimes they come, sometimes they don't. But when they do, it's worth the investment in time and money. Let's say you're launching a new product or service or opening your own company—make it a big deal! Create an event. Rent a large hotel conference room or a private party room in a restaurant. Invite giants in your industry. Invite happy customers. Invite the media from all over—blow your own horn and make them think they'll be missing out on a news scoop if they don't show up. If you're worried about the turnout, fill up the room with family and friends who will create a crowd and applaud and hoot and holler. Your new idea will seem like a must-have if you have people clamoring to get close.

If the worst happens and no one from the press attends your press conference, don't sulk away in defeat. Make your presentation, have a great party, and get it all on videotape. Then send the tapes out with a press release. Providing the footage and copy to the news crew increases the chance that you'll get on the air.

Once you set up the press conference, you can use that forum to piggyback for more exposure. When I had a press conference to announce an upcoming fight between Shannon Briggs and Lennox Lewis for the World Heavyweight Championship in 1998, I brought boxes of stuff to hand out: hats, posters, pictures, company brochures, media kits, press books, videotapes, and T-shirts. Lewis brought nothing. The press conference is exposure in itself, but here I have a room full of people in my industry—I'm going to exploit that opportunity. People clamored around Briggs to get their pictures signed and they left like walking billboards wearing "Briggs" hats and shirts. They had information in their hands about Worldwide Entertainment and Sports and many of the other athletes I represent. I think that to have that kind of forum and not take advantage of it is stupid—but nobody else does it, probably because it's very expensive and also because some say it's exploitive. Of course it's exploitive—that's the idea. People who don't like it should ask themselves why Lennox Lewis has no endorsement contracts. It has something to do with the way he's promoted (or not promoted).

Exploit all exposure opportunities by arriving prepared to flood any forum with publicity materials. Keep these materials in the trunk of your car at all times. It's much better to hand someone this information than to make a promise to send it later by mail.

Surfing for attention: Online advertising

I confess, I'm not on the cutting edge of high technology. I'm just finding out about the kind of exposure I can get by taking advantage of online advertising—and I'm finding out it's invaluable. There are so many people out there who are using the computer as their primary source for getting information and for communicating, I'd be crazy to ignore that kind of potential market.

My Web page lets the fans, athletes, and investors, as well as journalists, stockbrokers, competitors, and friends stay up-to-date on the company and our events. I don't mean to sound like a walking advertisement for the Internet, but it really is great for exposure. I've got links built in so people who visit my site can jump to a specific sport or a particular athlete. They can get information on the company and jump to our financial report; they can get a schedule of upcoming events and find out what happened at yesterday's event. They can see pictures of our athletes and send fan e-mail.

This is the kind of publicity I've been sending out in thousands of individual mailings (which I still do), but now I've got it all in one place for anyone in the world to look at when it's convenient for him or her. And it's a lot less expensive than my mailings. The best part is that now I can get this information to people who I would otherwise have no way of knowing are out there and interested! There's no mailing list in the world this large.

As a recruiting tool, the Web page often serves as the first point of contact for potential investors and athletes. Sometimes people hesitate to ask for information because they're afraid of announcing their interest. The Web page gives them a chance to anonymously take a look and find out what we're all about, and then they can decide if they want to take the next step by making personal contact.

To get an idea of how to use a Web page to advertise your company or service, visit my site at www.wwentertainment.com.

Become the center of attention: Party big!

Having a party is a great way to get publicity—if you do it right. When we throw parties, very often they're really just another kind of media event. I invite journalists from print and TV media. I invite big-name athletes, whether I represent them or not, because their presence draws attention to the event. I invite my clients, investors, and stockbrokers and tell them to bring their friends (who are often notable and/or wealthy people themselves). I invite my competitors and my enemies. I invite lots of people who want to party. I invite anyone who can bring attention to the gathering.

When Nike introduced its new brand, named Brand Jordan, named after Michael Jordan, Nike selected one of my star basketball players, Derek Anderson, to be the only rookie to endorse it and made the announcement at a press conference in New York City. The press conference alone gave Derek great exposure, but why stop there? This called for a celebration! We threw a party for Derek and invited everybody—all the important writers, reporters, and athletes from the press conference moved over to the China Club for our party. My clients, investors, and stockholders got to meet athletes like Vin Baker and Michael Finley; the press got to talk to a top-of-the-list group of veterans and rookies. And my company got terrific publicity. (Of course, I also had people giving out pictures of Derek, as well as my tapes, company brochures, and press kits.)

A party like that gives me immediate as well as long-term attention. That is the kind of event that shows our athletes how much they mean to our company and how we plan to take very good care of them. But also, because I invite people and athletes who are associated with competing sports agencies, I get a chance to show them what they, too, could be enjoying if they joined our team. And I know they leave the party and tell lots of other athletes and recruiters what they've seen.

Sure, I love a good party—but I really love the publicity it brings.

Whenever there's a reason to celebrate, party in a big way and invite anyone whose presence will be notable. Then call in the press to spread the word!

Give and receive: Community, charity involvement

Reaching out to the community and to charities is a sound and proven way to get yourself publicity. I first got involved in my favorite charity, Project Pride, because it was supported by a sports writer whom I trusted and knew was honest. Once I got involved in the work this volunteer group does with more than 15,000 kids, I was hooked. I just loved what they were doing.

When I make donations, or attend fund raisers, or bring my athletes to meet the kids, my name and my company's name have another outlet. I'm also very willing to respond to charity auctions that need donations. About once a month, we send sports memorabilia to an auction where the proceeds will be put to good use and at the same time Worldwide Entertainment and Sports will get another public forum.

It's also a very good idea to get involved in local service clubs and community work. Through these you're interacting with a lot of good people who each have their own network you can get involved in. Whether you volunteer at your kid's school, or coach a sports team, or join the library's fund-raising drive, you position yourself to meet people who can help you succeed.

The more you get out and meet people, the more people learn about you and your business. Join clubs, volunteer, socialize, shake hands. All these things are ingredients of success.

You *can* buy attention: Risk money, find a gimmick

We get an incredible amount of publicity, in part because we're willing to pay for it. We spend money on our athletes from the day we sign them. We treat them like gold; we take care of all their needs and we show them off with class and style. I think too many people wait until they have a winning product or service to start spending money to promote it. We risk money on the unknown to get publicity from day one. In the long run, this tactic pays off.

We invest in exposure constantly. We hold luncheons for sports writers and feed them steak. We host dinners for advertisers so they can meet our new athletes and offer them endorsement contracts. After the NBA draft in 1996, we threw a luncheon for Samaki Walker who was drafted by the Dallas Mavericks. We wanted everybody to know the name of our athlete. And we wanted more—we invited all the advertising agencies and the big shoe companies to our celebration at Elaine's in New York. When it was over, Samaki was in the news and he was lined up to endorse Apex sporting goods. We spend a load of money on things for long-term gains, and that alone sets us apart and gets us attention.

Publicity and marketing will take a big chunk out of your budget—but it's tough to make big money if you're not willing to pay for attention.

Constant, quality exposure is expensive, but you can also buy attention without a dime in your pocket. You can buy it with a gimmick. I don't think there's anything wrong with being outrageous to get publicity. Guys like Howard Stern and Dennis Rodman obviously feel the same way. I suspect they are both very smart men. Stern uses his access to the airwaves to grab attention with blatantly ridiculous statements and by doing "shocking" things, such as showing up to his New York book signing dressed as a woman. Rodman paints his fingernails, dyes his hair outrageous colors, and wore a wedding gown to his staged wedding—you bet he gets publicity. People like Stern and Rodman don't hurt anybody with their gimmicks, and they distinguish themselves from the pack of celebrities and athletes falling over themselves to get attention. It's obvious that the more people say they hate them, the more money they make. These men make millions and millions every year—you can't argue with that.

Make it happen

I know a lot of very smart people who don't get the point of publicity. They try very hard to do outstanding things so the press will notice them and give their work the attention it deserves. That's one way to get exposure, but too many absolutely great things never get noticed at all. I don't want to sit around waiting for somebody else to tell me my work is worthy of publicity. That's false modesty, and it's costly. I want to make things happen.

Take, for example, 17-year-old Casey Atwood, the world's youngest NASCAR driver and a very talented kid. We're looking for a corporate

sponsor for his car and we're not going to sit around hoping some corporation will notice him and make an offer. We're going to get his
name out there so that everywhere you look—there he is! He'll be the
biggest thing to hit the industry, and corporate sponsors will be falling
over each other to get their names on his car. So far, he's had pieces in
USA Today; he's been on the Internet on ESPN's SportsZone on a live
chat room; we're working with Jay Leno and David Letterman to get
him on TV; *Sports Illustrated* and *Sports Illustrated for Kids* want to
do stories on him. Casey's a young, all-American, bright, clean-cut kid
who's perfect for companies like LEGO®, Tommy Hilfiger, Toys "R"
Us. We're creating an image and the media hype behind it to get this
kid the corporate sponsorship for more than a million a year that he
needs—and it will happen because we will make it happen.

Anybody can market something that's already a winner. It's easy
to be retroactive, to pick up the phone and decide when to say, "No,
we don't want to do this deal," and "Yeah, we'll do that deal." The skill
is in getting publicity for the unknown and unproven. You have to
create the persona and aura about the person or product. Once you
get it, it'll stick.

---

*Getting exposure requires a proactive stance. No more sitting around
waiting—get out there!*

Looking on the bright side: Negative exposure

In the world of promotion, there's one thing you can count on:
When things go wrong, you'll get loads of negative publicity. When it
happens to you, try not to lose too much sleep over it—negative exposure is part of the territory. Even in the most scandalous circumstances, you have to remember that it's a long game and the public
has a very short memory. Something that's front-page news today will
be forgotten two or three weeks from now. What they'll remember is
your name. That's the up side: You got your name out there.

Bad news travels quickly—and is forgotten just as quickly.

You can also use publicity to counter negative news. If you think people may be hearing rumors about your company or if you're worried that a minor problem may get blown out of proportion, don't wait for it to happen—set the world straight. When Derek Anderson had a knee injury in his senior year at Kentucky that knocked him out of the top five NBA draft choices, some people questioned his durability. So before the draft, we got to work on building him up as a strong and healthy athlete with outstanding potential as a pro. We had pieces about Derek everywhere from *Inside Sports* to *Slam Magazine* and in all the local Kentucky papers (especially the ones in his hometown, Louisville) to create awareness that Derek's injury wasn't going to be a factor in his career. Derek was picked 13th in the draft and I think this massive predraft publicity had a lot to do with making sure he didn't slip out of the first round.

Even when things are going great, there will be people saying bad things about you. There's no way everybody is going to like you—especially as you get more and more successful. There are guys in football who don't like it that I'm also in basketball—so they bad-mouth me. Some basketball guys get upset because I'm in football—so *they* bad-mouth me. And the boxing purists who don't think I should be in anything but boxing really tear me apart. But am I going to hide or change what I'm doing just so I won't get bad publicity? I don't think so. There will always be people who are envious and jealous and people who decide to make a name for themselves off of your name. No matter who you are or what you do, you can't win with everybody. There'll always be people who will tell the press you're bad because you're young, or because you spend money, or because you haven't visited your mother this week! They'll say anything to make you look bad. Success will bring controversy and bad press; that's just the way it is. If they're not talking about you, good or bad, you're not even in the game. You're not making an impact. In fact, you should be more worried on the day they're not writing anything about you than on the day they're writing something bad about you.

Success will bring people out of the woodwork who will bad-mouth you. Enjoy it. It means you're a threat, and that's good. You should wake up every morning hoping somebody is talking about you—good or bad.

Get some help: Public relations

Taking time to promote myself and my business is absolutely necessary, but at the same time, I can't forget that time is money. If I spend too much time promoting, I could be losing money. That's why I've hired a public relations firm to handle publicity. I think this is a sound investment.

Good PR agents are well worth their fee because they have direct access to media outlets that serve your industry or market. Some PR people specialize in getting in gossip columns, others in fashion news, others in financial news. The agent for Worldwide Entertainment and Sports specializes in sports promotions; the agent for this book specializes in book promotions. These people have contacts and inside information that it would take me months to uncover. They identify the markets to target; they know how to reach your customers. They make up press releases, arrange for public appearances, compile press kits, contact reporters, and publicize important events. They put in the time that you don't have. All of this happens with one goal in mind: getting your name out there.

Name recognition is invaluable. It increases the likelihood that potential investors, clients, and customers will remember the company name and perceive it as desirable. This is worth the cost of hiring a public relations agent.

Getting your name out there is all about exposure. If you need clients, customers, or investors to be successful, you don't have a choice about this because the days of relying on word-of-mouth referrals to build your business are gone. Now we all need to sing and dance to draw attention away from our competitors and put the spotlight on our work. I don't mind; in fact, most of the fun we have is in marketing and advertising. The press conferences, the TV appearances, the parties, and so on all add enjoyable diversity to a business that in other areas can be quite cut-throat and stressful. Today would be a good time to map out a promotional plan that will take you to the next level.

Critical life lessons

✓ Identify the people in your industry who can get you exposure and keep in contact with them.

✓ If you haven't been in the press lately, make something happen and hold a press conference or write a press release about it.

✓ Recycle all good publicity: Send copies to other news regions and then gather the best into a press book to recycle again.

✓ You should cater to the public's need for visual promotions with highlight videotapes. Get your best on film, flood your prime market with your tapes, and follow up with phone calls.

✓ Never assume you can't get TV coverage. Get to know your local stations and reporters and bother them regularly.

✓ Use every opportunity to get advertising materials—press kits, shirts, pictures—into people's hands.

✓ You may very well be left in your competitor's dust if you don't get your name out on the Internet.

✓ Party big and let the world know about it.

✓ Charity work is good for your soul. It's also good for business.

✓ Be as outrageous as you want—as long as it's done with integrity—if it will get you the publicity you need to separate yourself from the crowd.

✓ Don't be afraid to risk money for publicity if you want to be a long-term player.

✓ Look for the bright side of any negative publicity and run with it.

✓ Sometimes it's best to let the experts help you out.

Pitch With Conviction

The term "pitchman" was used to describe street vendors who would yell out to passersby to try to sell their wares from street carts. Successful businesspeople are all modern-day pitchmen (or "pitchpeople," I suppose). They must use their pitch to convince investors, customers, and clients that their product or service is better than anyone else's on the street. They have to sing and dance to get attention and notoriety. The ability to give a good pitch is a strong indication of potential success.

Personally, I always give a sales pitch off the top of my head. That works for me. But I can't say that I'm making it up as I go along. I know my business and I know what I need from the person I'm talking to. The first rule of pitching is to have your thoughts and facts organized before you open your mouth. Whether you prepare for days or speak off the cuff, you have to be sure you can communicate logically, succinctly, and clearly. The death knell of any pitch sounds when the pitch begins to ramble or seem redundant. This type of pitch is insulting to the person you're talking to and takes up valuable time. So be prepared, have your facts in order, and know what you're going to say.

Preparing your pitch

There are many theories and ideas about how to give the perfect sales pitch. You can read books about it; go to seminars about it; attend classes about it. But in the end, you'll find that to make it work, you'll need to come up with something unique. Through trial and error, you'll eventually create your own style to convey your message. That said, I'll offer my two cents with an outline of a typical pitch I might give to encourage big investors to throw their money into Worldwide Entertainment and Sports. This example will give you an idea of how to organize your thoughts before you pitch. Generally, my presentation covers these six areas:

1. **Background.** The first thing I do is take people through my past, let them know where I've been:

   I've been in this business for 20 years. I've been a manager, a promoter, and an agent. I signed my first basketball player and boxer when I was 19 years old. In 1990, I was the first boxing manager ever to go public; since then, every boxing manager in the world has been trying to go public to get the capital, but none of them has been able to do it. Then, on October 22, 1996, I was the first sports agent to go public and I have raised $12 million, a testament to my business vision and credibility on Wall Street—a rare combination for a sports agent.

2. **Progress.** Then I'll talk about the progress I've made up to this point. It's important to show that you're moving forward, that things are much better this year than last year:

   Worldwide Entertainment and Sports became a public company only 18 months ago, but we've already raised close to $12 million with an IPO of $8.4 million and a private placement for $3.5 million. So now we have the money to blanket the country looking for the best. If we don't have the best people, what good would the $12 million do us? We couldn't have done better in these past 18 months: Last year we represented about five athletes; this year we have about 60. We have seven NBA players, including Bobby Jackson, the starting guard for the Denver Nuggets, and Derek Anderson, the starting guard for the Cleveland Cavaliers. (Derek has a multimillion-dollar deal to represent Nike.) They both made the All-Rookie Team, so we have two of the top 10 rookies in the league our first year in business, which is pretty incredible. Last year, we had three of the top 36 NBA drafted rookies. In football we have more than 25 NFL players. We have Antonio Freeman with the

*Green Bay Packers, O.J. McDuffie of the Miami Dol-
phins, Tyrone Wheatley of the New York Giants, and
Rickey Dudley with the Oakland Raiders. We just signed
Tony Hutson with the Dallas Cowboys (we believe the
best offensive guard in the NFL). He goes into free agency
next year and should make about $5 million a year. And
we signed Vashon Adams from the Kansas City Chiefs.
You know we have six boxers, including two of the
top-ranked heavyweights in the world: Ray Mercer, the
1988 Olympic heavyweight gold medalist and former
heavyweight champion, and top-ranked heavyweight
Shannon Briggs; and three of the top 15 heavyweights,
with Danell Nicholson (who represented the United
States in the 1992 Olympics).*

3. **Your vision.** You have to let people know where you're
going if you expect them to go along with you:

*I expect to make Worldwide the best full-service
sports and entertainment management company in the
country. We take care of athletes better than any other
firm; our mission statement says that when our athletes
retire, they'll never have to work another day in their
lives—and their children won't have to work either. We
also have the best people out there to service the athletes.
As the first public sports management company, we
have shown the vision to be pioneers in the sports agency
business. And now we're looking to buy other sports
agencies. It takes me just as much time to buy a whole
agency with an impressive client list as it does to recruit
one top-notch player. That's because there are hundreds
of people going after the players, but only a few people going after the companies. Did you know that one of my
competitors just sold his sports management company
for $120 million? With my business philosophy, we will
build a sports agency business worth a tremendous
amount more.*

4. **You and your track record.** This is a very important part of any pitch. It's the information that, even though you can't put it on a balance sheet, is invaluable:

> *I'm an ambitious guy. I'm not married; I don't have kids. I'm devoted to making Worldwide the absolute best. I'm out there working on this seven days a week with about three to four hours of sleep a night. I always do what I say I'm going to do. Everything I said I was going to do a year ago is happening now. And now I'm telling you I'm going to make you money. If you wait another year to invest, you'll see that I will have done everything I said I was going to do and the company will have reaped the benefits. Now is the time to get in on the ground floor and take the ride to the top. You don't want to wait a year and miss what's available right now.*

5. **Your backers.** When you're asking people to support you or your company, let them know who else has already signed on. We all like to know we're not going out on a limb alone. That's why it's so important to get a few very reputable and powerful names behind you. I've been able to get many credible people behind Worldwide. To mention a few, I might say:

> *I have a fabulous guy named Harvey Silverman on my board. Harvey, who is a senior partner of the very prestigious Wall Street firm Spear, Leeds & Kellogg was one of my original supporters.* Investment Dealer's Digest *recently wrote a great article about him and his partner, Peter Kellogg, saying that these multimillionaires head the company that controls more inventory in equities and options than any other market-making firm. I'm also supported by Ron Heller (one of the top stock brokers in the world) and Bruce Lipnick (a big-time money manager) who have both invested their own personal money in WWES. I've also been called on as a consultant for the Disney company on several occasions.*

6. **The benefits.** People want to be involved in things that benefit *them*—not you. Make sure your pitch explains what the person listening will get out of the deal:

> *When you buy into Worldwide Entertainment and Sports, you buy into a very exciting business. You own a piece of these outstanding athletes without spending $400 million to buy a professional sports team. When you watch them compete, you can root for them knowing that you're their backer. You can take your family to see this investment. You can take clients to meet the guys you support. I can make sure you get the best seats in the house. This is a great way to entertain clients—with front row seats at the fights. It's good for you and your son—something you can do together. This is a good way to meet other investors. There are a lot of personal perks to investing in this kind of company.*

Presenting your pitch

The content of your pitch is, of course, very important. The person you're talking to needs all the facts to make an informed decision. But the *way* you present an in-person or telephone pitch is either the glue that will seal the deal or the hammer that will smash it to bits. After all, you're not asking people to buy into only your product or service, you're asking them to buy into *you*. Don't hide behind the false belief that what you're selling is so good, it will sell itself no matter what you do or say. You're fooling only yourself. No matter what you're pitching, you yourself must appear to be a desirable product.

Look up and speak clearly. If you're pitching in person, you can't engage a person's interest unless you're making eye contact. And whether in person or on the phone, you've got to make yourself understood. Mumbling and low volume are sure signs that you aren't so sure about this deal yourself.

Appear confident. Never say, "I *think* we'll *probably* be able to...." Instead say, "We're *going* to do it. It *will* happen." Speak in definites. And watch your posture—body language has a lot to say about your level of confidence. Stand tall with conviction. If you slump forward, you give the impression of being unsure and hesitant. If you're not so sure about the chances of success, why should anybody else be?

Be enthusiastic. Don't confuse being low-key with displaying confidence. If you're excited about whatever it is you're pitching, show it! Show it in your smile, in your handshake, in your choice of words. Enthusiasm is contagious—go out and spread some around.

Be thorough. Want to blow a pitch? Come up short on the facts. If you have to say, "I'll look that up and get back to you," you might as well pack it up right then.

A positive, upbeat attitude is your best ally when you're making a presentation. Don't leave it home.

Pitching with your appearance

Your personal appearance is another kind of body language that speaks loudly before you get a chance to open your mouth. If you want to be listened to when you give your pitch, it's very important that you dress the part of someone worth listening to. It's not shallow to judge someone by their clothing—it's human nature. So look sharp no matter what it costs you. You can't ask for a million bucks wearing a $50 suit; it just won't work. The fact is, people like to give business and money to people they perceive as having already made it. They don't want to "gamble" on somebody who can't yet afford good clothes.

This doesn't necessarily mean always wearing a Brooks Brothers suit. Follow these two rules when you're dressing to give a sales pitch:

1. Wear what's appropriate for the setting. The business suit has its place in formal presentations, office meetings, etc. But the rule of dress says you should dress like the person you're pitching to. Find out what's appropriate before you go. If you know that the other person will be wearing a suit, wear a suit. If they will be casual golfing attire, wear casual clothes (that are new, neat, and pressed).

2. Whatever you wear, make sure it's top quality and in very good shape. Make sure nothing sags, wrinkles, is ripped, or shows wear. I'd like to think that this is understood, but I've been at too many important meetings where there were people pitching against me and their sloppy appearance alone knocked them down a few rungs. It makes you look lazy and makes it hard to believe you're a hard worker who pays attention to detail.

It always amazes me when people show up to present an important proposal wearing the same suit they slept in the night before. Clothes can talk much louder than words.

Take your pitch on the road

When you've got something to sell, you have to get out of your comfortable little environment. There are people all over this country just looking for someone like you to invest in. You've got to go find them.

Before you hit the road, map out a plan. It's a waste of time to run from town to town knocking on doors. You want to target your audience. I like to pitch to people who will at least open the door because of a mutual acquaintance. So I call everybody I know and ask them to tell me the names of people they know who might be interested in my pitch.

Right now as I'm working to raise money to expand Worldwide Entertainment and Sports, I'll call all the people in my own Rolodex, of course. But then I want them to lead me to other people. I'll call or visit all of these contacts, make my pitch, and then ask them who *they* know. I have no doubt the people I need to find are out there, and I won't stop until I find them. I have a great story to tell and I have a fabulous company. I just need to find the right investors. I have no doubt that I will because I won't leave any stones unturned in any state in the country—or in any country in the world.

I also use my network of friends and business associates to give me a prepitch buildup. Because I always treat people right and do everything I say I'm going to do for them, I can call in an occasional favor. So if I know somebody who knows the person I want to pitch to, I'll ask that person to pave the way. I'll call and say, "Hey, you've got to call so-and-so and tell him lots of good things about me. I want to get in there and give my pitch, but I need you to help me get my foot in the door." When you get a prepitch introduction, you go in with a huge advantage. The person has a personal recommendation about your track record and he or she knows something about why you're coming in. This is a lot better than having to go in cold. It increases your chances of success enormously.

If you really want to sell to all the right people, get out of town.

Getting an invitation to pitch

When you're trying to sell something, there's no such thing as "down time." Everybody you meet at any kind of function or event is a potential bull's eye. At business seminars, conferences, and workshops you can jump right into your sales pitch—but that's the only place where you have that freedom. At any other type of event, you have to be careful about bending everyone's ear. You can't stand on a soap box and gather everyone around to hear what you have to say. People hear business pitches all day long, from the door-to-door cosmetic lady to the telemarketers on the phone. They don't want to hear another one when they're out having fun. So at social events, your pitch has to come in the back door.

The secret is to get people to ask you, beg you, to give your pitch. Let's say I'm at somebody's house and we're watching a basketball game. I don't want to start talking business and get everybody annoyed because they can't concentrate on the game. But I will say something like, "Oh boy, I tried to recruit that kid. He was a tough one," or "I hope he plays well today. He's such a nice guy." Who could resist asking me to tell more? The natural response is to ask, "You know that player?" This is my opening to mention that I'm an agent and I have this company and we're looking to raise money and expand. Just conversation, but the subject is on the floor and now I can find out if there's anybody in the house who's interested in what I have to say.

Use whatever business you're in to get people interested enough to invite you to give your sales pitch. Let's say you're in the computer business. When the conversation turns to kids (everyone talks about their kids), you say something like, "Isn't it incredible how kids take to the computer? You should see this new program coming out." The natural response is to ask, "What program?" Now you've been asked to speak, and your audience is in the mood to listen. Too many people make the mistake of jumping into their pitch without an invitation. That's when you find yourself standing alone without an audience.

Another way to get people to listen to you when they're out of the office is to let them go first. If you want to talk business, but you can't seem to find an opening, get the people you're with to start talking about their businesses. That will open the door for you to follow their lead. It's easy to lead social conversation to business simply by asking, "What do you do?" (I don't lead with that question if I'm networking for contacts; it seems too obvious. But it's a good opener if my goal is simply to bring the conversation into the business arena.) Keep asking questions like, "That sounds very interesting. Tell me more about that," and "What are your plans for the future?" As you listen, you'll be able to tell if this person is the right audience for your pitch. If he or she is not, you've had a nice social conversation that can lead you to finding out who else this person knows who you might like to pitch to. But if he or she is the right person, you have the perfect lead: "Wow, I can't believe you do that. I'm in the such-and-such business and I've been looking for someone just like you." How nice to have someone else open the door.

Before you go into your song and dance, you probably should size up the situation. If you don't have time to give your pitch the forum it needs, or if you have a feeling the person isn't in the mood for doing any business, or if you're not fully prepared with all the facts, don't feel you must give your pitch now or never. Ask for a business card and tell the person that you have some business you'd like to discuss. Promise to give a call and then do it.

There are so many instances when your target audience may have been in the same room with you but you didn't know it because you didn't get them to talk about what they do.

133

Pitching to thousands

Presenting a pitch is usually thought to be a one-on-one situation. But it doesn't have to be limited to personal contact. Sometimes you might have something to pitch that can best be said to thousands of people through the media. This may be part of your promotional advertising plan (as described in Rule #9), but the media can also be used to pitch your latest idea and attract interest and attention for something that doesn't even exist yet. I might pitch an idea through press conferences or newspaper and magazine articles. Whenever I use the media to announce an event, an upcoming fight, a new athlete, an acquisition, etc., I make sure I also throw in a pitch for Worldwide as a public company with stock available. There's no way I'll let any news go out without mentioning the company, because I'm always making a pitch for name recognition on the stock exchange.

Another very effective medium that I've used to find a large target audience is fliers. If you're in computers, for example, make up fliers that carefully outline what you want to say and hand them out at a computer show. Or if you want to target a particular geographic area, put the fliers on cars in area parking lots, at train stations, in shopping malls, in office buildings. Or if you already have a specific target group you want to reach, you can send out your flyer through a direct-mail marketing campaign. Fliers can speak directly to hundreds of people you can't possibly meet personally.

The Internet has also become a place for big-time pitching. There are thousands of companies popping up that live or die on the quality of their online pitch. Why not be creative and use a personal Web page (with well-chosen links) to give your pitch?

Don't be shy about using these kinds of advertising tactics to pitch an idea. Just keep in mind that pitching to the masses should follow the same guidelines of preparation and thoroughness that you apply to personal meetings. Everything that has your name on it should be clear, succinct, complete, and accurate. When you've got your pitch down in an attractive and enticing form, don't hesitate to send it out.

Piggyback on pitch opportunities

When you get an opportunity to pitch your company or your idea, look for ways to make the opportunity pay off in other ways. Even if you don't sell what you're presenting, you're putting yourself in a position to meet important people. You're networking. You're making contacts that might help you meet some other goals. You should plan to bring home *something* positive out of every contact.

When I was pitching cellular phones when they first came out, I was the top salesman in the country. But this wasn't an easy pitch. First of all, no one had ever heard of "car phones." No one was sure they needed one. And they were very expensive—$4,000! But what at first seemed like a rather undesirable job was in fact a great opportunity. I was making a commission on my sales. I was given my own phone and free phone calls (which meant a lot to me because I was still trying to build my sports agency and was always on the phone), and I was meeting the wealthiest people around (who else would even consider paying $4,000 for a phone?). In fact, selling the phones became a pretext to meet influential people. Later, I went back to those same people to ask them to invest in my sports management company. Some of them are still my best investors. Because they remembered my pitch, my enthusiasm, and my personal presentation, some of them were willing to see me again.

I had the same attitude when I worked on the commodities floor of the New York Stock Exchange. I knew that wouldn't be my life's work and I knew I wasn't going to strike it rich there, but I used the circumstance to meet big investors who I would later contact to invest in my sports management venture.

To this day, I never leave a meeting where I'm pitching without leaving some door open. I recently gave my pitch to an influential investment banker, Adrian McKay, at the firm Furman Selz that usually does deals in the hundreds of millions of dollars. He liked what he heard, but thought that Worldwide was still too small for his company. I told him that even though he couldn't do anything for me immediately, today, I was really glad we met. "When we meet one year from now," I told him, "You'll see that everything I told you today about the future of this company will have come true. You'll see that this is a company you can count on to keep its promises." And now, I'll be keeping in touch with this man. I'll be keeping him updated on what's going on. I'll be keeping him interested in following our growth. Before you know it, he'll be jumping at the chance to finance me for tens or hundreds of millions because he will have watched the way we work and will see that I've done everything I said I would do.

The point is, even if you can't sell whatever it is you're pitching today, leave the door open for keeping in touch. This lets you build up credibility and increases your chances of making the sale somewhere down the line. This is your biggest asset when your company is young.

Critical life lessons

✓ When you open your mouth to try to sell something, you're giving a pitch. Make it logical, succinct, and clear.

✓ When you give a pitch, think before you speak. Cull out the highlights of your background, your progress, your vision, your track record, your supporters, and the benefits.

✓ When you personally make a pitch, you can't hide behind high-gloss, professionally prepared graphics, handouts, and posters. You have center stage. Make sure you're a desirable product.

✓ Tell people, "Why wait for tomorrow when you can do it today?"

✓ Your appearance speaks louder than your words. Make sure it says good things about you.

✓ Prospective customers and investors don't all live in your neighborhood. Get out of town and meet them!

✓ At social functions don't make a bore of yourself by bending everyone's ear with your pitch. Instead, use social conversation to get others to ask you to "please" tell them more about what you are selling.

✓ In addition to personal-pitch meetings, take advantage of the media, Internet, and promotional fliers. These are tools you can use to pitch to thousands.

✓ Never leave a pitch meeting without taking something positive with you—whether it's the name of an important contact, a promise to be in touch in the future, or an idea for another project.

Follow Success

From where you stand right now, look ahead to the next level of accomplishment. Find ways to surround yourself with successful people on that level. Their positive attitudes are contagious, their knowledge is priceless, and their business and social contacts are the rungs you need to climb to meet success.

There's an old saying, "You're known by the company you keep." I believe this is true. So if you want to be known as a successful person—find a way to get yourself into the company of people who are successful.

Success breeds success

There's no replacement for knowing your stuff and working hard. Given that, being in an environment with successful people automatically increases the likelihood that you will be successful, too. It just makes sense. Successful people are positive and optimistic, whereas 99 percent of the rest of the world is not. When you spend time with people who are upbeat and action-oriented, it boosts your own energy level and increases your desire to be just like them. When you hang around with people who have worked hard and made it, it makes you more ambitious. It provides a constant reminder that it can be done. This alone is reason enough to surround yourself with successful people.

Successful people are can-do people. They don't sit around talking about what needs to be done—they're doing it. When you spend time in their company, you take on this same approach to life.

I could destroy your chances for success just by putting you in a room for two weeks with a group of pessimistic people. If you sit from 9 a.m. to 5 p.m. every day with people who are constantly complaining: "This project will never get done right"; "I can't possibly bring in this account by the end of the month"; "life sucks"; you'll be negative and pessimistic, too, and there's no chance you'll make it big, because if you're hanging around with wanna-bes who complain all day long, you'll become just like them. But if you go somewhere that's full of can-do people who are full of vigor and optimism who say, "I don't care what he says, I'll get it done"; "there's got to be a way around this problem, give me some time and I'll find it"; "isn't life great?" you'll come out feeling like you could conquer the world. And that's the feeling you need to be very successful. Because attitudes are contagious, I don't keep people around me unless they're positive and optimistic.

It's key to surround yourself with optimistic people who believe in themselves, who are positive, who are achievers, who are goal-oriented. This assures you'll be the same.

Build mentor relationships

Building a mentor relationship creates an opportunity to be in constant contact with a successful person who can teach you what you need to know to rise to the next level of success. If you'd like to get involved in a close teacher/student relationship, follow these steps:

Step 1: Identify who can teach you what you need to know.

When I was taking my company public, I met Morty Davis of D.H. Blair Investment Banking Corp. I knew right away that this was the guy who I wanted to teach me about the business-end of things: about how to take my company public, about financing, about how to make money in the market. Because one of my goals is to be one of the richest people on earth, if I see a guy who is a self-made billionaire, he's the guy I want to be my mentor. What are your goals? Who has already done that? Who can teach you the ropes? The answers to these questions will put you on track to pursue a mentor relationship.

Step 2: Find a way to get close to the person you've identified as a desirable mentor.

I found out quickly that there are thousands of people who want to get close to Morty Davis, so I needed an in. One of his brokers was a friend of mine, so that helped me get at least one toe in the door. My friend told Morty that I was a hard worker; I was honest; I was going places; etc. Now at least Morty was hearing from an "insider" that I was someone worth giving a little time to. Little did Morty know that my goal was to make me his personal hobby. Once you've identified a potential mentor, find a way to get close. (A little later, I'll give you a few ideas about how to get to know successful people.)

Step 3: Find out what your prospective mentor likes.

I found out that Morty loves boxing (lucky for me), so I invited him to a match. I also learned that he loves hamburgers far more than a thick steak, so I invited him out for dinner and arranged with the kitchen to have a hamburger ready even though it wasn't on the menu. These things let important people know you're really interested in getting to know them better.

Step 4: Prepare to pay "tuition" for your mentorship.

Surrounding yourself with successful people can be expensive. In my case, once I got to know Morty very well, he was kind enough to invite me along when he traveled. My education at his side took me all over the world to places such as China, Africa, and Israel. The opportunity to spend so much time with someone like Morty was too good to pass up—but it wasn't cheap. It cost me $10,000 to $15,000 a trip to travel first class with Morty Davis. But I still say it was a great investment. He's helped me earn that amount a thousand times over. He's taught me things I could never learn in any business class. Morty has let me sit in on his business meetings; he's shown me how he structures deals; he's opened up to me and taught me things that most people don't have access to. These things are priceless.

Step 5: Use what you learn.

When a mentor opens up to you, that's only half the value of the relationship. You have to take the information and use it. Use not only the factual information, but also the day-to-day business stuff that plays a big part in success. Watch how this person meets people. How she treats people. How he networks. How she negotiates. How he stays motivated. Take advantage of every minute you're in the presence of your mentor.

You are known by the company you keep

Earlier, I told you about my personal and financial relationship with Harvey Silverman in the chapter about networking. He is the man who sent me a quick $60,000 when I asked him to invest in my brand new company. At the time, I had no idea that he was one of the most successful guys on Wall Street, and I didn't see him as a potential mentor for quite a long time. I didn't do my homework right away and investigate who this person was and what he had done that I could learn from. Then about a year later, he asked me to bring some of my fighters over to his place for a little get-together. As soon as I saw his place, I started getting the hint that Harvey was a big fish—it was a luxurious penthouse in New York. Finally, I started checking into who this guy was and it was immediately clear that Harvey had influence that could bring me to the next level.

I started going to Harvey for business advice (and I increased the amount of money I asked him to invest). Once I figured out how unbelievable this guy was, I increased how often I kept in touch. It was not only the money that Harvey could give me, but I realized that by association with him and his company, I could gain unshakable credibility. Spear, Leeds & Kellogg (Harvey's company) is one of the most prestigious companies on Wall Street, which, as reported by *Investment Dealers' Digest*, controls more inventory in equities and options than any other market-making firm. Harvey taught me how to leverage my position using his name.

When you choose a mentor, make sure it's someone who has a reputation that will help you, not hurt you. When I was shopping my first public offering around, people were very pleased to learn that Harvey was on my board of directors. They were impressed that he was my mentor and that he had invested his money and his time in me. Harvey and his company are known for being clean, prestigious, and above-board. My association with Harvey gave people the same impression of me. That's what a mentor relationship should do, so choose carefully.

> *You surround yourself with successful people for the same reason you
> want to play tennis or golf with someone who is better than you:
> These people motivate you to do better. If you hang around only with
> people on your own level, you'll never rise above them. If you want to
> be a millionaire, associate with millionaires. Then when you're a
> millionaire, find billionaires to hang out with.*

Finding the rich and famous

To surround yourself with successful people, it is definitely who
you know, not what you know that pulls it off. Here again, networking is key. You may not know a whole circle of people on the level
above you, but you must know one person, or you must know someone who knows someone. Once you decide where you want to fit in,
network like crazy to meet people who can introduce you to other
people. Sometimes these people will be among your own circle of family and friends. Sometimes they'll be people you meet through your
charity and community involvement. Often they'll be contacts you can
make through your business associates. Map out a plan of contact.
Who will you build relationships with and where will they lead you?
(See Rule #4.)

Get to know the gatekeeper

Once you decide who you need to know, you have to figure out a
way to get yourself into their inner circle. Most very successful people
don't answer their own phones at work or have their home numbers
listed with directory assistance. They are intentionally unavailable. I
recommend infiltrating their outer circle first. Get to know the people
who have their ear, the people who protect them from intrusion.

When I decided that I wanted to know Morty Davis and be in his
circle of associates, I quickly found out that all calls and inquiries
went through Morty's right-hand-man, Marty Bell. To get to Morty,
you had to get through this person who everyone warned me was a
tough businessman. His job was to keep people away from Morty and
he took the challenge seriously. Rather than trying to "get past" this
kind of gatekeeper, I realized I'd do better getting to know him. When
I would call Morty's firm to ask questions about my IPO, I didn't ask

for Morty (who I wasn't going to get anyway), I always asked to speak to Marty. I built a business relationship with him by respecting his position and knowledge. I didn't brush him off as a lackey and insist on going right to the top. Marty was smart and very helpful. Soon we were arranging luncheons and dinners. I used these as opportunities to find out what he liked, about his family and his hobbies. I learned that he had a son who would love some sports jerseys and other sports stuff. I found out that Marty liked to go to basketball games. This information gave me an avenue to drive right into his circle.

It turned out that Marty Bell was a great guy and it was easy to become good friends. When Marty went on a trip with Morty, he invited me to go along. I was now in a position to get to know Morty who I knew had so much he could teach me. It took me a long time to get to know Marty and Morty, but it always takes time to meet the best.

Don't try to brush past the gatekeepers—stop and get to know them. Make them your first line of contact and let them lead you to the person you really want to meet.

Tap into client contacts

You have business access to your clients every day. You have a reason to invite them for dinner. You have opportunities to get to know them. Now find out who they know. For every client, there are endless contact possibilities. If a client invites you to her kid's graduation party—go! You have nothing to lose and everything to gain in contacts.

My clients are my athletes and they are often a source of contact for me. I spend so much time with them, giving advice, guidance, and support, but I don't want to forget that they have lives outside of my circle with access to many wealthy and influential people. (I'll even ask my athletes to keep their eyes open for people I should know.) It was Shannon Briggs who introduced me to a prominent Fortune 400 young guy who's worth hundreds of millions of dollars. We've been meeting socially on and off for about six months and our friendship is just now starting to gel. He recently told me he wants to put a million dollars into my company. Obviously, for me, client introductions are a great way to meet very successful people.

Attend charity auctions

Charity auctions attract successful people who like to donate big-ticket items. I look at the auction list and if I see, let's say, that they're auctioning off a vacation at a major hotel chain, I'm going to find out if the hotel owner is at the auction. If he is, I want to say hello. What a great way to socially meet very wealthy people!

Finding the people you want to meet isn't that hard. I get to charity functions early and ask the head waiter to show me the seating chart. (I'll say I can't find my friend and want to find out where he's seated.) I look for big names and find out where they're sitting and go over and introduce myself. (I have to confess: Mitch Modell taught me this move.) If you are not too pushy and if you don't try to monopolize the evening, most highly successful people will be gracious enough to give you their attention for a few moments, just long enough for you to introduce yourself and promise a follow-up contact. Say something like, "It was very nice to meet you, and if you don't mind, I'll drop you a note during the week. There's something I'd like to discuss. Have a nice evening." Then follow through and keep in touch.

When you meet the right people, promise some kind of follow-up in the future. While the event is still fresh in memory, write a note or call to talk. Meeting successful people is only half the quest; getting to know them is the real challenge.

Meet the best at seminars and conventions

Going to seminars, trade shows, and conventions is a great way to meet important people. Key people in your industry will be the speakers, and the audience is full of positive people who are looking for ways to improve what they do. I want to meet these kinds of people. I also know that this is a captive audience interested in my product—what a perfect opportunity! While you're there, stay alert to opportunities. Eavesdrop on conversations. Find out who's sitting to your left. Who's in front of you? These events pull like-minded people into one place—you'll be surprised who you may bump into.

Don't limit yourself to events in your own industry. If it will help you or your business to socialize with people in the newspaper or publishing industry, go to workshops for journalists and attend seminars for columnists and editors. If that's where you'll find the people you want to get to know—go there! If you hear that a big-name in a particular business (someone you think can bring you in touch with other big people in that industry) is teaching a course at a nearby university, see if you can sign up as a nondegree student. Many successful people share their knowledge in public forums. Many of them are registered with a speakers' bureau who will tell you their schedules. Dig. Investigate. Find them.

You can't get to know successful people if you don't know where they spend their time.

Be in the right place at the right time

Successful people aren't going to come to you. They don't knock on doors to invite people out to dinner or for a spin on their yacht. You have to ask yourself, "Where are successful people?" and go to those places. You can start by looking in expensive restaurants, in first-class seats on airplanes, in country clubs, in the front seats at sporting events. Go to awards dinners and shows. When you make up your weekly schedule, be sure to arrange engagements in places where you can expect to see important people. You may not meet the one who is interested in striking up a conversation the first time you splurge to be near them, but this is a long-term tactic that eventually pays off. If you consistently put yourself in the places where you're most likely to meet successful people, you will eventually find some who are talkative and open to new faces. But even with receptive people, a single meeting isn't worth much. Get the name and location of their business so you can get in touch in the future. And then find a common interest, such as golf or art or sports, that will put you in contact again, and then again and again.

At the end of each week, make a list of everyone you've met. Then prioritize those you want to make an effort to meet again. Concentrate on a few people at a time so you don't send out a hundred follow-up notes with no time to keep track of what happens after the initial contact.

Critical life lessons

✓ You are most likely to meet your potential if you surround yourself with positive, optimistic people.

✓ Tune into the winning attitudes and can-do beliefs of successful people; they are contagious and motivating.

✓ Keep yourself wide open for learning opportunities with successful people. Create for yourself a mentorship with a person who has already done what you want to do.

✓ You can gain status and credibility by associating with the right people.

✓ You'll get where you want to go much faster if you don't try to push your way to the people on top. Find out who are close to the people you want to meet and get to know those people first.

✓ The very successful people in this world will not come to you to offer their help. Identify places where successful people go. Go there. Meet them. Get in good with them.

Keep Your Eyes Open

*Look back over your life at the really important things that have
happened to you. You'll find that many of them weren't planned
or calculated. You didn't wake up one morning and say, "Today I'm
going to go out and land the account that will change my life."
Or "Today I'm going to fall in love." Many key events in your life
happen by chance. That's the most exciting part of each day—you
never know what the day will bring.*

When you get up in the morning, what's the first thing you say to
yourself? If you mentally collect where you are and what day it is and
then say to yourself, "Oh man, the same old, same old," you're defeated before you even start. You've got to get up every morning ready
for new and exciting things that you can't possibly know anything
about yet. That's how life is if you're open to it. You never know
what's just around the corner.

Wake up

I get a kick out of people who sleep until noon and then complain
that nothing exciting happens in their lives. You have to *make* something happen; you have to get up and milk every day for what it's
worth. I figure there will come a day when I'll get a billion years of
sleep so I'm not going to waste too much time on that now. I need
every possible minute of every day to make things happen and then
watch where they lead me. You should wake up every morning looking forward to the things you know nothing about yet. That's what
makes life exciting.

I'm not saying that good things will happen to you just because
you wake up early, especially if you sit in your room all day. You create the unexpected by going places and meeting lots of people. You

have to put your nose into every situation that's open to you. The more often you do this, the more likely you'll find yourself in a position to take advantage of something great that you weren't even looking for. It's through these efforts that you get the most life-changing surprises.

Keep your eyes open so you'll be ready to take advantage of the surprises life hands you every day.

Be alert

We all have business and social activities that we pencil into our appointment books and attend for specific purposes. Some people might go to a seminar to learn a new technique of management. Some people might go to a wedding to socialize with seldom-seen family members. Others might go to their kids' athletic events to cheer them on. One day rolls into the other with these kind of events. If you go to these functions with your eyes and ears open, you'll quickly find that they'll bring you daily surprises. There are opportunities sitting in everything you do every day; it's up to you to uncover them.

Soon I'll be attending a social function that will not be the social highlight of my year, but is something I wouldn't miss—it's my camp reunion. People have said they're surprised I would go to a camp reunion because I have so many other "important" things going on. You've got to be kidding! Where else can I meet so many successful people and have a common point of conversation? There will about 250 people there, and you can be sure I'll know the business background of every one of them before I leave. Here I sit having no idea what the night will bring, but because I'm going with my eyes open, I have no doubt that I'll get something very positive out of the time I'll put in.

Wherever you go, look around—who else is there who you can meet? What other objectives can you meet? What's going on around you? This is how you make your own luck. You'll find yourself saying, "Wow, I can't believe little Billy's coach is the purchasing agent for the company I'm trying to sell to!" "I just found out that Aunt Sally's second nephew is looking for a small startup company to invest in!" You just never know until you dig.

I'll meet with anybody. Let's say on a slow day, somebody calls and says, "Hey, my brother's in from out of town and I'm taking him out to lunch. Why don't you join us?" Well, this isn't the most exciting invitation I've ever had, but if I have no other plans, I won't turn down the invitation cold. I'll ask a few questions to help me decide if this is worth giving my time to. How do I know who this brother is? What contacts can he pass on to me? How we can work together on something special? Not only does the brother offer possibilities, but just getting out puts me in a position for things to happen that wouldn't if I sat home or at the office. I might meet somebody walking down the street whom I haven't seen in a long time but would love to get to know again. I might meet somebody at the restaurant. Who knows? That's the exciting part of every day—if you put yourself in the position to take advantage of surprises.

I remember the time I was at my table at the China Club (I always reserve a long table for friends who might drop by) and this guy I never saw before sat down. I'm sure he didn't realize it was a private area of the club, but instead of asking him to leave, I started talking with him. It turned out that he loved boxing and invested a substantial amount of money in my fighters and has become a close friend. I love that kind of surprise.

There's no such thing as being "too big" to meet people. Your local butcher could have a cousin who could make your day. You just never know.

Be flexible

People often get caught up in their own little schedules. They leave no room for a stop at the bathroom, never mind an unscheduled adventure. If a tight schedule keeps you from getting out and doing things in other environments, it's holding you back. If you're not reaching your goals, change what you're doing. You've got to leave room to deviate from the daily grind and live a little. Meet people, let your hair down, have some fun. This is not just advice for personal well-being; it's advice for business success. If you do these things in the right environments, you'll be putting yourself in the position to make things happen—things you can't predict.

You also need to stay mentally flexible. Sometimes our minds get stuck in a kind of tunnel vision that keeps us from seeing the many opportunities that lie just outside the path we're on. Say, for example, you go in to talk to someone hoping to convince him or her of one thing and quickly realize that that's not going to happen. You have to be able to switch mental gears and see what unintended benefit you can bring out of the meeting.

To switch directions like this, you have to stay mentally flexible. If I had ended the conversation when I realized he wasn't going to be investing, I would have lost out on what looks like a very interesting relationship. There's no way you can predict what might come out of every conversation, every meeting, everything you're involved in if you're mentally flexible enough to grab the unexpected. No way.

Create your own luck

You can't sit in your office waiting for great things to happen. Get out; be involved in life. You'll find that you suddenly get very lucky. You start making connections that bring you big opportunities. Join country clubs, take up golf or tennis, vacation at upscale resorts. You become who you hang out with. (See Rule #11.)

You'll also make your own luck by thinking creatively. Give yourself the time and freedom to explore life. Is there a class you've always wanted to take but didn't want to indulge in at the expense of time you could be spending on business? Go do it and consider it a good business investment. Bill Gates and Paul Allen, the cofounders of Microsoft Corp., met in school; you can't know what might come of it until you try.

When I think back looking for an example of when I was "lucky," I think of finding the greatest football agent in the world, Joel Segal (who has become president of Worldwide Football Management). Once I decided I wanted to open a football division, I started looking for a talented agent. I put out feelers. I told lots of people to keep their eyes open for me. I started scouting other agencies. But when it happened, I didn't wake up that morning saying, "Today's the day I'm going to find the best football agent in the country." It happened when the phone rang and my friend Gary Scharf said, "I have a guy I want to introduce you to." I had laid the foundation for this to happen, and then the best just fell into my hands.

I was also "lucky" when I found my attorney, Herb Kozlov. Herb represented boxing manager Bill Cayton when Don King convinced Mike Tyson that he should manage him instead of Bill Cayton, and again recently when Bill sold his fight-film library to Disney in a $100-million-dollar deal. When I was first getting my game plan together to take Worldwide public, Bill told me over and over that I should meet this great lawyer. Finally, I went to him to review some boxing contracts. As we talked, it turned out that he did SEC deals and registrations for IPOs. When I went in, I had no interest in changing lawyers, but by the time I left, I was very happy that I had found Herb, and I handed the whole package to him. Now Herb is on my board of directors and is the second-largest shareholder in the company. This person who is now an integral part of my life was someone I expected to do just a small piece of business with and never see again. Because I'm always out talking, working, and meeting people, I can expect something big to happen at every turn—I just never know what it will be.

You have to be opportunistic if you want to find life's opportunities.

"Lucky" people jump into life with gusto. They know they are in charge and that they can make things happen. For them, life is not a passive activity. They actively try to squeeze every bit out of every day. It's not a coincidence that these people are the ones who are most often pleasantly surprised by what life hands them—unasked, unsolicited, unexpected. Plop. Right in their lap falls a great deal. Out of the sky drops a windfall of good fortune. The truth is, it just looks that way. In reality, because these people are always active and involved, they are creating the opportunity for good things to happen.

I remember the day when I was down in Florida and Mitch Modell invited me to dinner to meet a very successful insurance agent, Tom Cundy. I didn't know anything about this guy; I didn't have any immediate need to meet an insurance agent. But I went anyway. When we arrived at the restaurant, Mitch introduced me to Tom, who turned around and introduced me to Joe DiMaggio! I couldn't believe it! I went to have dinner with an insurance agent and the next thing I know, I'm having dinner with the biggest living legend on earth. Since then, I've become good friends with both Tom Cundy and Joe DiMaggio and I know that if I had turned down that dinner invitation, I would be kicking myself to this very day.

Life can't surprise you if you don't give it the chance.

Look for the bright side

When you keep your eyes open for opportunities, don't overlook the fact that you can find them in negative circumstances as well. Not everything that happens today will be great. But keep in mind the axiom, "You just never know," and remember that something good can come out of even the worst circumstance.

You can create your own positives if you have the right attitude. Think of any awful circumstance (excluding death) and see if you can turn it into a positive. If you break your leg, you can probably use the rest and the time to reflect on where you're going in life. If you lose an important client, use that as motivation to go out and get two even better clients. If you keep your mind open to the positive possibilities in every circumstance, you'll find that life suddenly seems to go your way. (See Rule #3.)

Just ask Shannon Briggs. When he lost to Darroll Wilson in a major, nationally televised fight on HBO where Shannon was also featured in a five minute profile, it was a blessing in disguise. At first, there was no way we thought anything good was going to come out of that. But by keeping our eyes open, we found that this loss gave Shannon the opportunity to fight George Foreman. Foreman was looking for somebody he could beat; if Shannon had won the Wilson fight, there's no way Foreman would have agreed to take the risk and fight him. Then, because Shannon won the Foreman fight and received great press all over the world for weeks afterward, he was in a good position to fight Lennox Lewis for the World Heavyweight Championship title. One thing just led to another in ways we never could have foreseen. That's the way some of the best things in life happen.

Critical life lessons

✓ Life doesn't make house calls. You have to get out and meet it face to face.

✓ The harder you work, the luckier you get.

✓ Life is full of surprises every day. Get out and look for them.

✓ The key events in one's life often grow from unplanned and unexpected circumstances.

✓ Put yourself out into the world so it knows you're alive and looking for action.

✓ Tunnel vision drastically reduces the possibility for a positive outcome in any life circumstance.

✓ Make it a rule to meet everybody and anybody you can. You never know where the acquaintance will lead you.

✓ Most often, "lucky" people create their own luck.

✓ Life can hand us unwanted and problematic surprises. Accept them graciously and find a way to turn them to your advantage.

Know How to Negotiate

Negotiation has lost its true meaning in the business world. Too many people go to the negotiating table ready to battle for a victory. They celebrate their ability to slip in a quick point unnoticed. They look for openings to take advantage of the "opponent." But when you're in your business for the long-haul, you've got to remember that to "negotiate" really means to "compromise." The goal is to have both sides walk away happy and stay happy.

Negotiations are a major part of my business. On any given day, I'll be negotiating contracts between Worldwide Entertainment and Sports and new athletes, between my athletes and their teams, or between the athletes and companies asking for endorsements. These experiences have taught me how to come away from the negotiating table a happy man.

What do you want?

You should begin all negotiations with clear and precise negotiating goals. Before you meet with the other party, decide exactly what you *must* have. There are probably lots of things you'd like to have, but what is it that you must gain? Having this down in writing will keep you from being distracted or flustered by the small stuff. Always set your bottom line before you begin negotiations.

When I negotiated for the WBC Heavyweight Championship fight for Shannon Briggs, my number-one goal was to make sure I came out with the agreement that we would get this fight. There were a lot of people negotiating to fight the heavyweight champ, Lennox Lewis. So when I went in to meet with Lewis's managers and promoters (Pat English, Dino Duva, Panos Elidas, and Frank Malone), I knew in advance that because I was going in as the challenger, I was going to make everything as easy and as simple as possible. Sometimes people argue over nickels and dimes and make a pain in the ass out of themselves. But I wasn't going to haggle over things such as free tickets or rooms, first-class airfare, the penthouse suite, or options on the fighter. I gave in everything—I just wanted the fight. I figured when we won, then Shannon would be the champion and I would be in a position to ask for the moon. But right now I wasn't going to lose sight of what I wanted by getting caught up in unimportant details. The Lewis camp probably left that negotiating session laughing that I could have squeezed out so much more: an extra 20 tickets, or a couple more airline tickets, or the penthouse suite. I didn't care—I just wanted the Heavyweight Championship fight where, if worse came to worse, I would make only a couple million bucks. Nobody took advantage of me. I came out with exactly what I went in looking for.

When you're the underdog, the less haggling the better. I'm sure this strategy helped us get that fight. I knew the other fighters and, more important, I knew the managers and promoters who were negotiating for them, and I knew they would argue to the death on the little issues. All things being equal, why not go with the guy who doesn't drag out negotiations for weeks over the small stuff? This works for me all the time.

Prioritize what you must have and don't lose sight of it in the heat of negotiating. Stay focused on the big picture and remember: Negotiating is a game of leverage. If you don't have the leverage, don't quibble.

Know the other guy

Before you head into a negotiation, learn as much as you can about the person with whom you'll be negotiating. Just as my athletes and coaches invest hours studying, analyzing, and strategizing over videotapes of their opponents, I do similar research on the people with whom I negotiate. You should try to uncover the other person's key needs and criteria—it may not be money. Lots of people bargain for power, distribution channels, or access to powerful people. This knowledge gives you more to bring to the give-and-take of negotiations. Maybe you want more money and you know the other person wants media exposure. Maybe you can use that information to close a deal that meets both of your needs. I remember an instance when I was negotiating with Wall Street bankers. I was able to get a better deal by offering the people with whom I was negotiating access to the athletes—the opportunity to take their own clients out to dinner with big-name athletes was something they wanted badly. This was a perk I brought to the negotiations that gave me some leverage and made both sides happy.

There may be an instance when, after a little research, I might find out that a general manager's job hangs on his ability to get a top player under the salary cap. I could go in and say, "That's not my problem. This is the money I need and I don't want to hear any excuses or I'm taking my player to another team."

But because I'm in this for the long term, I want to build relationships with the general managers. After talking to my player, with full disclosure and, of course, the player's consent, I may have to defer a little money for the good of the team and to help the general manager do his job. This isn't really a sacrifice or a giveaway; this will help me and my player in the long-run when we're at the negotiating table again.

When you're negotiating, don't focus solely on what you want. You have to understand what the other side wants, too. This helps you bring more to the table to bargain with.

Always do thorough research before you agree to negotiate. Read everything you can and surf the Internet for news and insights. When possible, speak to people who know the other party.

This is another area where networking comes in handy. Because I have befriended the four largest professional boxing promoters in the world, I can pick up the telephone any time, day or night, and get information about what their adversaries are doing. This lets me go into a negotiation for a fight knowing where everybody stands.

If you have a complete mental picture of the people with whom you're negotiating, you can better bargain for the best deal for both of you. When my executive vice president of marketing, Ryan Schinman, and my CEO of basketball, Erik Rudolph, were working a deal with Converse for Bobby Jackson (Denver Nuggets), they had a lot of research to do before showing up at the meeting in Boston. They knew Converse is a publicly traded company, so they went on the Internet to get the up-to-date stock price; they found out from other agents what their athletes were getting to endorse Converse products; they investigated to find out what other athletes signed with Converse and who else they planned to sign to see if it made sense to add Bobby. They learned who the decision-makers were at Converse so they were sure their meeting was scheduled with someone who could seal the deal without sending Bobby up through layers upon layers of people. They found out how the basketball shoes perform, and they got the facts on national and worldwide sales and Converse's plans for the future. Knowing all this before going in to negotiate gave my team the upper hand. They knew what they wanted and what Converse would be willing to give. By the end of the meeting, Bobby Jackson was the national spokesperson for Converse sneakers.

Find out what other deals these people have done and what their needs are at the moment. No matter what field you're in, everybody's got a hot button you should know about. Maybe you're negotiating with a guy who absolutely needs the deal, or with a guy who could take it or leave it. If you're making a million-dollar deal with a billionaire, he couldn't care less if you get everything you want and will drop negotiations at the first sign of haggling. But if you're working a deal that will make or break the other party, that opens a whole other kind of negotiating session. I always want to know if the person with whom I'm negotiating has the ability to walk away from the table.

When I was buying my condo in Florida, I knew that the developer hadn't even broken ground on the building yet and he wasn't going to get financing unless he had a certain amount of deposits. This knowledge gave me the upper hand to make a fast deal. I told the seller that I had to get back to New York and was going to buy something, somewhere before I left. I took out my checkbook, and I wrote out a check for a 20-percent deposit on an amount I wanted to pay and left. Knowing the builder's situation told me that it would be tough for him to turn down money-in-hand from somebody he knew he was never going to see again.

When you're working on a deal that's really important, look to the experts to do your research for you. There are searches that will bring up everything about a person, from traffic violations to jail time, from drug offenses to birth certificates. You can find out anything you want to know—for a price. Ask a lawyer about doing a background search—ask for an overview of the kinds of information you can obtain and how much it will cost you. When the deal is really big, the extra time and money are worth it.

Find out about the person's temperament. Will he explode and throw you out of the office if you haggle too much? Will he drag things out just to frustrate you? Does he work fast? Is he honest? Does he expect you to attend meetings in a tie or dressed casually? Does he want to meet in a fancy restaurant or in a coffee shop? You should know these things.

You can also use the information you find during your research to flatter the other person and to create a positive atmosphere. It's helpful if you can throw out little pieces of information during your conversation, such as: "I know you're a pioneer in this field." Or "I know how hard you worked to get yourself through such-and-such college." Or "Your financial report for last year was very impressive." Or "I'm sure the people who benefit from such-and-such charity are very grateful for your generous contributions and personal involvement." These kinds of comments eased into conversation let people know you've done your homework. You can also use background information just to be nice. If you find out the person with whom you're negotiating was recently honored at a dinner by a community organization, get a hold of the program and have it framed as a gift. Or if you come across a picture of the person in the news, track down the original and have that framed. These are little things that get big results.

Negotiate face to face

It's always better to negotiate face to face rather than over the telephone or through go-betweens. In the first place, you get a lot more accomplished. I've had deals go round and round for weeks on the telephone. Then we finally agree to get together in one room and a few hours later, we're done. It's human nature to be more direct, more open, and more willing to give and take when you can look someone in the eye. Negotiating face to face is especially advantageous when there are lots of people involved. If you're talking with lawyers, and accountants, and spouses on the phone, weeks will go by before you get a response to one question. Get these people together and get it over with.

When you negotiate in person, you can also watch body language and reactions to see how serious the other person is. I can tell in two minutes if a person is serious when I see him in person. But over the phone, I can't see expressions; I can't see the smirk or rolling eyes. I can't look him in the eye.

Every move you make in face-to-face meetings has something to say about your position in the negotiations. What do you lose when someone intentionally keeps you waiting? What do you gain if you intentionally keep someone else waiting? These little maneuvers are all about power. If I want to bring a guy down to earth and deflate his ego a bit during a meeting in my office, I'll take a short phone call. That action says I can take his deal or leave it; I'm not champing at the bit. That's why I know if a guy takes a phone call when I'm in his office, he's not too serious about the deal. After one or two calls, I've been known to get up, say, "Call me when you're serious," and walk out the door. Sometimes the person will stop me and apologize and hold all future calls. Sometimes he won't. This says a lot, too.

Use the home-field advantage

It's always advantageous to negotiate on your own turf. This is absolutely true for the same reasons all sport teams fight all year to establish home-field advantage. You automatically have leverage. Whether I'm in my office sitting behind my desk or in the back of my limo working out a deal, I have the home-field advantage. Being on the home field is a psychological thing that gives a sense of power, because people start out a little intimidated when they're in unfamiliar surroundings.

If you've agreed to meet in a neutral place, such as a restaurant, make a quick move to pick the place. Make it the one where you've

spent time building up a reputation as a valued customer. You bring
the home-field advantage with you when you walk in and are immediately shown to *your* table and are greeted by the owner. I recently
went to dinner with a banker and a potential investor. This wasn't an
official meeting, just a chance to get to know one another (an important preparatory step in negotiations). I invited along a few friends
to make the evening fun and relaxed. I brought them to my favorite
restaurant, knowing I'd be treated as if I owned the place. This atmosphere gives me an aura of importance and accomplishment that is
priceless in business deals.

Come in strong

Before you head into a negotiation, take a good look at your position. Is it strong? If you're going in with an ace in your hand, shoot for
the moon. When I take Antonio Freeman, the top NFL wide receiver,
to free agency, you can bet I'm going to aim high. You never know
who's going to bite. But if you're not feeling strong when you go to the
table, you'd better find some way to build up your deal.

Playing one side against the other is one way to put yourself in a
position of strength. When Nike wanted Derek Anderson to endorse
their shoes, Converse also wanted him. This gave us some leverage.
When we went to the meeting with Nike, we knew they were feeling
nervous—they brought in Michael Jordan and Phil Knight to personally talk to Derek. And naturally, they had to offer more than
Converse. I don't know if Nike knew exactly what Converse was offering, but they knew an offer was on the table from a bitter rival and
that's all it takes. In your negotiations, try to get some other party to
make an offer. This gives you leverage to get what you really want
with the best party.

Sometimes you have nothing to come in strong with. In this
case, negotiating can be like playing poker. You have to create your
strength—sometimes by bluffing. If you don't have the cards to
win, pretend you do: "We just got a call from someone else and they're
drooling over this deal. If you don't want it, just say so." And remember to be kind about it: "I want to work with you, but I also have
to protect the company and do what's best for my family. I have to
take the best offer." This puts a little pressure on the other side. It's

always to your advantage if the party with which you're negotiating believes there's somebody else ready to jump into this deal—now! You're playing one against the other, and sometimes the "other" is a bluff.

Obviously, I'm not going to give the details of the deals when I bluffed, but I can say that I never made a deal by bluffing that didn't make both sides very happy. Sometimes when you're sure the deal is good, you have to stack the cards in your favor a bit, just to show the other side how right the arrangement is for everybody.

This works both ways, of course. The other party will also be trying to convince you that there's someone sitting in the wings waiting to sign if you don't. I don't think I've ever bought a piece of real estate without the agent telling me, "We have an offer coming in on this property in an hour." This is too obvious and I can see right through it, but in other situations, it's sometimes hard to tell. You have to size up the situation and the experience of the person with whom you're negotiating to decide if you can believe him or risk a bluff. That's another reason to do background research before negotiations begin.

You should also come to the negotiating table mentally strong. Always go into negotiations with the appearance of strength and a take-it-or-leave-it attitude—even when you're down and desperate. If you're behind on your mortgage and your credit cards are maxed out, don't say so. Give the appearance of being stable and strong. Unless you're a young person working with an older, wealthy mentor, you never want to approach a deal from a position of need. Don't say, "I need this deal or I'm going under." People don't want to sign a contract with someone who's on a sinking ship. An admission of weakness takes away tremendously from your ability to negotiate anything in your favor. They'll look down on you. They'll assume you're not successful. They'll know you're someone who can be taken advantage of. Down-and-out people don't get sympathy, they get screwed.

Never show a position of weakness—ever. The more needy you are, the more time you should put into looking like you're on top of the world. Wear the best clothes, shine your shoes, stand tall, and smile.

Don't go first

An age-old rule of bargaining says: "Don't be the first one to name a price." Let's say I want to buy your car. It benefits me for you to tell me how much you want for the car. Your figure may be lower than the figure I have in mind. I have nothing to gain and everything to lose if I say the price first. This often creates a tug-of-war at the negotiating table. Everybody knows you don't want to be the first to name a price, so the victory goes to the one who has the skill to get somebody else to do it. You can frustrate the person into breaking down and giving a figure if you act like you're unsure, hem and haw a lot, and keep beating around the bush: "Gee, I'm not sure. Golly, I just can't put a figure on it. Oh, I don't know. What do you want for it?" You can also frustrate the seller by implying that finding the right figure will take a long time and delay negotiations: "I've got to think about this and analyze it. I want to call my lawyer and my accountant and my actuary to see what they think. Do you think you could meet with them, too?" You also can sometimes get a price on the table by being persistent. When I was younger, I'd bother people so much by calling and calling and asking them what price they wanted for something, they'd finally give in and name their price. People respect perseverance (and they'll also do anything to get rid of a pest). Tell them, "Give me a starting point."

Sometimes you may find yourself in negotiations with somebody who's really good and is not going to name a price first. If you really want that deal, you'll have to put a dollar amount out there to move things along. That's when it's time to throw out a very low number. Force the person to move you up to something more realistic. If he or she won't, it's time to take action. Take out your checkbook and say, "Okay, I'm ready to close the deal. I'll make this out for X dollars. Okay? Here you go." Sometimes they'll take the check and sometimes they won't, but at least you're moving forward.

Get all you can get now

When you size up the situation, decide how much you can get without blowing the deal. Is the person anxious to sign? Is this someone who admires you and trusts you? Can you draw up an honest and sound contract that will cover you both down the line? Don't assume the circumstances will be the same at any time later on. Take whatever you can get now.

The other day, I was talking with a boxing manager who was negotiating a young boxer's contract and he reminded me how important this piece of advice can be. He told me that he was offering the kid a five-year contract. I told him to make sure he put in options for another five years when this contract expires. "No," he said, "I'm just gonna do the five years. The kid loves me; he'll sign with me again." This is crazy. When you negotiate you have to use every advantage you have right then and count on nothing in the future. Right now, the kid would sign anything the manager put in front of him; he needs the manager 50 million times more than the manager needs him. That's a lot of leverage that should be used to make a sound contract. The manager won't have that leverage five years from now.

I told him, "The boxer is 23 years old, so he'll be hitting his prime just when the contract is up. If he ends up being as successful as you think he's going to be, he's gonna be making tens of millions of dollars and he's not going to be hanging around with you so much any more. He's going to be out with his entourage, celebrities, and big shots. He's going to get advice from all kinds of people telling him to forget your name and find somebody better. Or let's say he stays loyal to you, how much do you think he's going to want to re-sign when the contract is up? He'll want you to take less of a percentage or he'll want a million-dollar bonus—something. Now, when you have the leverage, is the time to put in the option for an additional five years. Don't be stupid."

Get it while you can. Don't assume anything will fall into place when the contract is up.

Make the money real

Talking about money is like playing at a casino with chips; you don't really feel like it's money. I've seen guys throw down $10,000 worth of chips like it was nothing—these are the same guys from whom I couldn't get $20 out of their pocket. When you're negotiating, the same thing can happen. You talk and talk and it becomes too easy to throw around dollars and terms. Bring those terms into reality—

have your checkbook ready. Or even better, bring a pile of cash. Nothing like good ol' cash to move a deal along. Now the negotiation isn't a game. I've been known to do this, and let me tell you, I usually get the deal I want—it's hard to argue with cold cash.

Consider the risk/reward ratio

In any negotiation, you have to give something to get something. That's what negotiating means—finding a compromise. But with this give and take comes risk/reward considerations. Are you willing to risk the loss of something you want to gain something else? People who get recruited to work for other companies are in this risk/reward situation all the time. They go into negotiations and find they're being offered more money. That's the reward, but what's the risk? Maybe they're not getting the same stable work environment or support staff. These things have to be weighed in all negotiations. People in sales face risk/reward decisions every day. Are you going to sell fast and get out of there before things break down, or are you going to sell quality and stick around for repeat business? Even in your negotiations with customers or clients, you have to consider risk and reward: What if you're selling computers to a person who knows nothing about the product and you realize you could charge triple the value of the computer? That would be the reward, but what's the risk? The risk is that someone might educate this person and you'll lose the account down the road. You've also given out written proof in the invoice that you're a crook—this news will spread fast through your industry. Rip him off now for quick gain? Or be fair hoping it will pay off in the long run? That's a risk/reward decision salespeople make in their negotiations every day. When you go in to negotiate a contract, you'll be faced with the same kind of decisions. You should know in advance what you're willing to risk.

There are two schools of thought on risk/reward ratios: 1) Take as much as you can upfront for immediate profits, or 2) Be fair and expect it to pay off in the long run. I recommend going for the long term if you plan to stay in the business.

This risk/reward consideration played a big part in the negotiations between Antonio Freeman and his team, the Green Bay Packers, when he was a restricted free agent in 1998. (A refresher in lingo: As a restricted free agent, a player can give up his contract with his team and negotiate with another team, but if another team signs him, that team has to give up things such as first- and third-round draft picks.) Knowing that in 1999 he'd be a free agent (able to sign with any team without these restrictions), and therefore much more valuable, we told Green Bay that if they offered him enough in 1998, he'd stay—but otherwise he'd stick to his old contract and be gone the following year. The Packers called his bluff by offering only $18 million. To be honest, I thought we were going to take it. But the day of signing, Antonio decided, "Forget it. I'm going to take the risk and go for free-agency next year." This was a risk for two reasons: 1) His present contract gave him only $1.5 million, and 2) Football contracts aren't guaranteed. So if Antonio got hurt, he wouldn't be worth much on the open market when he does became a free agent. But on the other hand, if he has a good year, the rewards will be great. He'll be open to $35- or $40-million offers (with a $10-million signing bonus). Big risk—big potential reward.

Time is money

In lots of negotiations, both sides throw out ridiculous terms and then spend weeks and weeks coming back to where they both knew the deal should have started to begin with. I don't like this approach. I want to make it clear what I need or what I'm willing to offer and talk seriously. With people I know and respect, I'll say: "You and I both know that if I haggle over this deal for another week, I could get more out of you, but I like doing business with you and I have other things to get to, so I think what we're looking at is fair for both of us. Let's close it now." If I negotiated another week or two, I'd probably lose out on some other deal going on someplace else, and still come back to the same deal that was on the table to begin with—no better, no worse, just the same. Time is money in most businesses, and that has to be weighed into your bargaining plan. How much do you lose by spending too much time on one deal? I close more deals because I don't drag things out and annoy the other party. There are lots of people out there who don't need my business. If I were to go on and on and delay and delay, they'd have no problem saying, "You're a pain in the ass. I'm taking the deal off the table. Don't bother me again." I've done the same to people who try to drag things out on me.

Because time really is money, always give the other party a deadline. It tells the other person you're confident, serious, and don't have all year to dicker over this deal. The message should be, "Let's do it and get on to new business." Without a deadline, it's human nature to put a deal on the to-do pile intending to get to it tomorrow. There's no pressure. Everybody's busy with lots of other things, but whether it's a day, 10 days, or a month, everybody should know that at some point, the deal is off.

Think before you jump

When I was younger, I was so anxious to get things done, I would agree to almost anything that looked good at the first meeting. Now, I never say yes during the first meeting. I've found it's much better to say, "Things look good; I just want to think about it overnight." Nobody will ever blow a deal or lose respect over that. But you will get yourself in to trouble and blow future opportunities if you agree to a deal on the spot, go home and start having second thoughts, and then call back the next day and try to change things around. Nobody likes somebody who changes a deal.

Even if you're 100-percent sure you want to do it , always sit on a deal until the next morning. There's several advantages to this:

1. Taking time to think keeps you from looking too anxious. You always lose negotiating leverage if it appears you have to have the deal.

2. Taking time before committing gives you a chance to run the deal by your mentors and people you respect to get their advice.

3. Snap decisions can come back and hurt you. Thoughtful ones rarely do.

All the way around, it's to your advantage to hang back, ponder, and analyze the deal.

Only when there's a real possibility that someone else could beat you out of the deal between that moment and eight o'clock the following morning, should you make a decision on the spot. In most instances, nothing will happen overnight.

Think long term

Whatever tactics I might use, I always try to negotiate a win-win situation so both parties walk away satisfied with the deal. That's key to developing long-term relationships. Maybe you can screw somebody for a couple thousand dollars, but after you pay your taxes on it, what's the big deal? It's not worth the cost in the loss of future business. If you get a reputation as a con man who can't be trusted, you've screwed yourself out of a future in the industry. This is a small world, and in each particular business, it's even smaller, so don't think that anything that happens at a negotiating table is a secret. Always assume that everybody at the table will be telling at least three other people about you. Hopefully, they'll be saying that you're tough but fair. I'm always looking to make a great deal, but I don't want anyone to regret working with me. Each side should come away feeling each has gotten the best deal possible. I'm a long-term player who isn't going to rip anybody off. All my experience and advice center around this point.

If you're a long-term player, you're going to see the person with whom you're negotiating again and your reputation and future standing in the industry depend on your negotiating style.

Critical life lessons

✓ A negotiation is a compromise—not a battle for victory.

✓ Always know your bottom line before you begin negotiations. If you come out with nothing else, at least you'll come out with that.

✓ Face-to-face meetings on your own turf give you an automatic advantage.

✓ Find out the priority needs of the other person and use them to bargain for your needs; also use them to make sure the other side comes out feeling they got what they wanted.

✓ Even when you're the underdog, you've got to find something that gives you a strong base to stand on.

✓ The person who puts the price on the table assumes the weaker role, so don't go first.

✓ Cold, hard cash slapped down on the table will move even the slowest negotiations toward a final deal.

✓ When the reward looks terrific, be sure to analyze the risk that goes with it.

✓ Time is money, so don't bicker over the small stuff.

✓ If you "sleep on it" before you sign, you'll be more confident it's a good deal.

✓ People who are in business for the long haul make sure that both sides walk away happy from the negotiating table.

Work a Room

You can do great things for your business when you're out having fun. Go to weddings, sporting events, bat mitzvahs, cocktail parties, fund raisers, class reunions. Have a ball and bring home a load of business opportunities.

Some people call making social contacts "working a room." I guess that's a good description, because when I go into a room, I do get right to work. If you're hesitant about using social functions for business purposes, get over it. In a social setting, you catch people outside their office environment when they're not in their business frame of mind, and that's the best time to make business contacts. There's no way I'd sit in a corner with my close friends and ignore the possible contacts all over the room.

You have choices to make when you're out socializing: You can stay tight with a few close friends all night, you can stand by the bar white-knuckling a drink hoping someone says something to you, or you can put on a friendly and aggressive personality and go out and meet people. It's your choice.

The benefits of mixing business with pleasure

If you want to be successful, you can't be afraid to introduce yourself to strangers. You have to know how to meet people and make them feel good. If you can do that, you will reap many, many benefits. What follows is a list of some of those benefits.

✓ People in high places respect your attitude. They see you're ambitious, hard working, and aggressive.

✓ People think you're smart. You automatically take on the aura of business smarts when you move around and work deals in any environment.

✓ You make great business contacts and connections that can bring you and your business to the next level.

✓ You create ways to follow up with important people during business hours.

✓ You build a reputation for yourself as someone who's going places.

If you don't learn how to mix business with pleasure, not only do you lose out on these benefits, but you gain a bad reputation. If you're sitting in your chair hoping someone will come up to you, you may be doing it because you're shy, but to other people it looks like you're rude and cocky. Let's say you're in a room with a load of successful, influential people and you stay glued to your seat. People will look at you and say, "What's the matter with this guy? He could be having as much fun sitting at home in front of the TV."

You may be holding back because you're afraid of making a fool of yourself, but here you are making a fool of yourself by sitting still. I'm not saying it's easy or it comes naturally to everybody, but it's something you can work on. Start with your attitude. When you're going into a social situation, remember to bring an attitude that conveys concern and caring for other people. Show a warmth that makes other people open up to you. Combine this with a positive outlook, a good sense of humor, charisma, energy, enthusiasm, and a sincere interest in others. Now you're gonna make something happen.

Once I was at this big social function that was full of very snobby people. I saw this guy who was being ignored and so I went over and introduced myself and tried to make him relax a little. We talked; we laughed. The next day, he called and told me to call his friend who is a big money manager and who loves boxing. I called the guy up and before I knew it, he put $60,000 into WWES. Being kind to someone who looked a little uncomfortable certainly paid off.

> *"Sincere" is a key word in building the right attitude. It's easy for me to spot people who are faking it. They shake your hand while their eyes roam around the room to see who else they want to "get to." They laugh too loudly at nothing. They say hello with a painted smile and then have nothing to say. People have to feel you genuinely like them.*

Preparing to make the most of socializing

Before you even show up at a social gathering, you should think ahead about how to get the most out of the event. What do you want to get out of this? Is there anybody in particular you know you want to meet? If it's a required function (such as a company retirement dinner) forget that you'd rather be doing something else and focus on the opportunities that will be out there. You'll never get to sit and chat with the president of the company during business hours—but you can at an event like this. Take advantage of that.

Do your homework. If you're going to a function sponsored by an organization, find out in advance all about the organization so you can ask informed, intelligent questions in your conversations. It's not impressive to say, "So tell me, what does this organization do?" It's much better to say something like, "I read that your charitable contributions were up last year. To what do you attribute that?"

Sizing up the room

When you arrive, hold back before you walk through the room. Get a look at who's already there and where they are. Look for who you know. See if anybody you know is talking to somebody you want to know. Try to position yourself for the best proximity to people you want to meet. Once I went out to dinner with my buddies Tom Cundy and Mitch Modell (and about six other people). Among those people was Cundy's friend, Joe DiMaggio. In my book, nobody's bigger than Joe DiMaggio. He's a living legend. So naturally, I was excited, but when we were shown to our seats, I found myself at the far end from DiMaggio. I couldn't stand this—I couldn't hear what he was saying and I couldn't get to know him from where I was. So while I was looking for a way to get closer, Cundy's granddaughter (who was sitting next to DiMaggio) got up to go to the ladies' room. I jumped up and sat right in her seat and stayed there for the rest of the meal.

Nobody said a thing and when the girl came back, she just sat in my seat. (She was so young and so familiar with Joe DiMaggio that the switch meant nothing to her.) If I didn't get up out of my seat, it would have been a whole different night for me. Sitting next to DiMaggio gave me the chance to get to know him and for him to get to know me. Since then, we've socialized and become good friends. This wouldn't happen today if I hadn't decided what I wanted and made a move to get it.

There's a big difference between having dinner with someone when you're at the far end of the table and when you're up close— a big difference.

When you size up a room, don't make the mistake of automatically delegating *anyone* to the bottom of your priority list. Assume everyone there you haven't yet met is a heavy hitter until proven otherwise. The worst dressed person, or the one with poor language or social skills may end up being the wealthiest and most influential person in the room. Let's say you're sitting at a table at a wedding reception with people you don't know and all evening you ignore the shy, socially awkward guy sitting on your right and give all your attention to the charismatic, well-dressed guy on your left. Won't you be the loser when the bride explains to you a week later that she sat you next to "that shy guy" because he's one of the wealthiest people in the world and she thought you'd appreciate the personal contact. If you slight people you don't even know, you always risk insulting someone who could have been very important for you to know.

Don't stereotype people. Assume everyone is important until proven otherwise. Meet them and decide for yourself if you want to keep in touch.

Know the pecking order

Before you barge onto the scene, you've got to know that there's a pecking order in working a room. The more influential people wait for the less influential people to make the first move. If I'm at a place where I know I'm higher in that order than a person at the next table (meaning he wants to meet me more than I want to meet him), then I wait for him to come say hello to me. If the night is almost over and he still hasn't said hello, then I'll probably make the first move to say hello. I have to figure that maybe he doesn't yet understand the way the pecking order works. I'll say hello and expect that eventually he'll realize he should have come to me first.

On the other hand, there may be heavy hitters in the room who will wait for me to come say hello to them. I'll definitely do that. If I get distracted and don't get to an important person for an hour or two, I make sure I apologize for the delay. I'll say, "Don't ever think I wouldn't come over to see you. I would never be in the same room with you and not come over. How are you?" I don't want them to think I'm the putz who doesn't know the order of things.

Sometimes you might have to make a quick decision about who to give your attention to first. Let's say that, at the same time, you see your good buddy who you haven't talked to in the longest time and an important person with whom you'd like to do future business. Who do you approach first? I have to go with the business contact first—again that's the pecking order of things.

Once I was at the C^2 restaurant in the China Club (which I co-own) in New York when my partner and friend introduced me to two very special people: Jules Haimovitz (president of King World, which distributes big shows such as the *Oprah Winfrey Show* and *Wheel of Fortune*) and John Schneider (the managing director of Allen & Co. While we were talking, I saw a good friend who had been down-and-out lately and who I wanted to talk to so he knew that I wasn't one of those "friends" who was going to ignore him when he was down on his luck. I caught this guy's eye and gave him a discrete hand motion that let him know I wanted to talk to him. Then, later, I made sure I found him and let him know how important and special he is to me. I made sure, even though it took some time, that I got to talk to that friend like I promised.

Decide where you stand in the pecking order and make your move to first approach every person who stands above you. In the end, make sure you've said hello to everyone.

Get to work

When I work a room I want to meet two goals:

1. Make every person I know in that room feel special.

2. Meet as many important people as possible.

To meet my first goal is easy. It's fun to work a room full of people I already know.

I think the people who go into a room and feel awkward are too worried about what other people will think of them or say about them. I don't worry about that because I'm going to go right in and tell people what I think of *them*—and it's always positive. Right away, I want to make each person feel special: "Your last deal was great." "Only you could do it." "You're the best." I compliment everyone with superlatives.

The last thing you want to do is to offend somebody you know by not saying something nice, or worse—not even saying hello.

To meet my second goal is a little harder, but it's still fun. First, I have to identify who the "important" people are. This is why if I'm going to a party or a club, I go early to talk to the maître d' and ask to look at the seating charts. I want to scan the names. I remember spying someone I wanted to meet at Rich Rubenstein's wedding at the Pierre Hotel. (Rich and his dad, Howard, run a world-renowned public relations firm whose client list reads like a who's who of famous people.) Being in the wedding party gave me a good opportunity to look over the crowd. The whole night, I knew I wanted to meet Leona Helmsley; so when I saw a time when she was free, I went up and introduced myself. It would be inappropriate to arrive at her home or her office and do that, but it's perfectly acceptable to introduce yourself to anybody in a social setting.

I have to say that I learned something else by making the move to meet Ms. Helmsley. I learned that I shouldn't listen to what other people, the grapevine, or the media say. Despite her reputation for being "mean," I found Leona Helmsley to be a very nice and gracious person. I told her that if she were a man, she'd be considered a genius. I believe that. So don't be put off by other people's impressions. Find out for yourself. Lots of times it's just jealous and envious people talking. Go right up and say hello and make your own decision.

If you walk up to influential people when they're working out at the gym, or as they're leaving their office, or when you see them walking down the street, they'll look at you like you're nuts. They'll grunt a greeting and turn away. But if you say hello at a social function, you're both there with a common bond and it's easy to talk.

Another way to get to know people is through a mutual friend. Don't be afraid to ask a friend to say nice things about you. Say, "Hey, you've got to put in a good word for me with so-and-so. Tell him I'm really sharp and I've got a good business going. Tell him you want to introduce me." Your friend will do this if you ask. But if you just stand around hoping the mutual friend will make the contact, you'll probably go home disappointed.

Getting friendly

The initial hello tells you a lot about your relationship with people. You might go up to someone you think you have a great relationship with and he or she will barely give you a hello—then you would know that relationship isn't so strong. Somebody else you think doesn't like you very much will give you a big bear hug and bring your relationship to a whole new level. Pay close attention to how people return your greeting.

Your first personal contact during an introduction is the handshake. Make it count by making it a two-step process: 1) Shake the hand; 2) Look the person in the eye. I'll never understand people who shake my hand while looking someplace else. Eye contact is such a simple thing, but it's so important. These people spend loads of time and money going to workshops, and seminars, and conferences to learn how to do well in business, and then they let their eyes roam during a handshake and blow the whole thing. Always put the two steps together if you want to make a sincere and lasting impression.

The handshake should be firm. Don't squeeze to break knuckles and don't grab just the fingers. At an initial meeting, leave it at that. You have to know somebody for a while before you give the handshake with the pat on the back or the covered handshake with the left hand placed over the clasped hands.

Greetings that include hugging and kissing require more thought. In social settings it's perfectly acceptable (and sometimes expected) to hug and kiss business associates hello—but you have to be able to make a good call about the timing. Is this person at the point where you'll get an embrace back, or are you still six months away from that point? If you initiate an intimate greeting and the timing isn't right, you'll embarrass yourself. You should never look for a kiss or hug at an initial introduction. Let the other person initiate it.

The way you say hello to people has a lot to do with how they'll respond to you. Give a firm handshake, look the person directly in the eye, smile, and give a compliment. It's simple, but so few people do it right.

Conversation starters

What do you say after, "How do you do?" This is the moment that will determine if you're going to shine or sizzle. In my opinion, I don't think you should *start* a conversation with a personal question. I never ask, "What do you do?" or "Where do you live?" They are just too common and can cause very successful people to take offense (they might think you should already know or that it's none of your business).

To successfully begin conversations, I tap into my ability to size up people and their interests very quickly and then I make sure I'm up-to-date on news topics. If the person is wearing a Yankee hat, go with that: "I think the Yanks are looking good. I saw today that the mayor says he wants them to stay in New York." If you see a reserved "suit," try talking finances: "Wow, did you see the market today? The options moved three points!" The possibilities are endless if you keep yourself well-read. Before you arrive, take a look at the day's newspapers for topics of conversation. Check out the headlines, the business news, sports, and life-style sections. You'll be ready for anyone you meet. (If you find yourself in a social setting and you are not up-to-date on current events, you can play it safe by talking about wherever you are: "This is a great restaurant. When I ate here last week, I had this shrimp dish you should try. It was terrific.")

Let's say I see George Steinbrenner at a social function. I don't know Mr. Steinbrenner personally, but obviously I know what he does and I want to meet him. I'd go up and introduce myself and open up a conversation about his field. I'd start with a whole list of superlatives and then I'd ask a question so he couldn't just nod his head and walk away. I might say something like, "I think you're one of the greatest owners in the history of baseball. Your desire to win is unparalleled. You're the hardest working owner in sports. Let me ask you, when you bought the Yankees for such a great price back in the late 60s, how much competition was there? Was there a lot of bidding going on?" This guarantees he'll have something to say back to me. The conversation won't end with a "How'd you do?"

Of course, you do want to know what people do, so if you don't already know, keep the conversation going until they reveal something about themselves without having to ask them directly. By talking about your own hectic work day, the person you're talking with might then offer, "Oh, I know what you mean. I was overseas all week working to get my line of clothes picked up by a Chinese distributor and now I'm so far behind." There you go—she's into retail clothing overseas. I put together clues throughout the conversation; it's more fun for me that way and it keeps people from getting turned off by what can sound intrusive. (This is especially true for very successful people who are always on guard against people trying to worm their way into their network.)

On the first go-round, I don't ever try to talk business right away. The initial conversation is purely social and complimentary. It's the time to ask how the other person is doing and relate a quick story about a mutual interest. If I know there's something I want from a specific person, I'll do the short-chat, introductory routine first, go away and talk to other people. Then I'll work my way back. "Oh, by the way," I'll say, "you know that deal you've got going? I'd like to get involved in that. How about we talk about it? I'll give you a call tomorrow." It's very rare that someone in a social setting will turn you down.

Conversation starters help you to get people feeling relaxed. They're not intended to pave the way directly into a business deal. Be patient.

Rejection

Every time you put yourself out and offer your hand with a self-introduction, you're taking a risk. The person may or may not welcome you. If you get rebuffed, don't take it personally. It just goes with the territory. But as you climb the ladder, you will see the odds change. In the beginning, you might score on a social introduction one out of 10 times. As you get more successful, you'll move to three out of 10. And by the time you're really successful and your reputation precedes you, you'll make important contacts about seven out of 10 times.

Regardless of how many times you meet with a cold fish, don't let it throw you. Just move on to the next person. There are lots of other people you can give your time to. Figure, "Well, there's one rejection; now the law of averages says I won't be rejected again for a while."

You can calm the stress of a bad contact by saying to yourself, "Gee, it was about time a rejection popped up. I was due. Now I'm not due again for a while."

Making your exit

If you meet someone with whom you would like to keep in touch, ask for a business card before you move on. Gather as many cards as you like, but make sure you have a plan for using them constructively. I collect cards for two reasons: 1) To feed potential investors and customers into my mailing list, fax list, and Web site address list. This data base of contacts is invaluable to me. These are people who I've met, who now know my name and my business, and who I can easily keep in touch with through mailings. And 2) To follow up. If it's a really important person, I'll follow up with a phone call and invite him or her somewhere: "Do you want to go to a fight? A game? What do you want to do?" That's how I get to know people. I like to first meet them in a social setting and then continue that social atmosphere at our next meeting. (See Rule #15 for the details on entertaining for business purposes.)

Personally, I don't give out business cards at social functions. I don't think it's productive for me. People stick it in a pocket or wallet or on the table and forget about it. So I don't give out cards. But I do *take* cards—discretely. This way, I can control the follow-up after the initial meeting. I go home and send out a nice note saying how nice it was to meet and I enclose a company brochure and/or a videotape about Worldwide Entertainment and Sports. This way, they get information about me and my company in their office environment when they're in the mood to think about business. The chances of my card making into their Rolodex is much greater than if I handed it to them at a party. Then I make sure we remain in touch. If I've made an important contact, I'll follow that up with a phone call. But if I give out my card, I'm stuck waiting to see who's going to move first.

Don't give out your business card to everybody in the room. After you talk and decide that this is a person you'd like to know or do business with, ask for a card. This puts you in charge of the follow-up.

In social settings, it's inevitable that you'll run into somebody who will get your ear and not let go. You've got to deal with this aggressively or else you will end up stuck in a corner all night and miss out on an opportunity to meet other people. To prevent this, if I'm with somebody, I always set up a signal system. Before we go in, I'll tell my associate, friend, or date: "If I catch your eye and you see me pull on my earlobe, come over and say, 'Excuse me, but I've got to take Marc away for a minute.'" (Obviously, now I have to think of a new signal.) If I'm on my own, then I have to cut the conversation short myself, trying to be polite but also blunt if necessary. I'll say something like, "Excuse me. I don't mean to be rude, but I've got to see someone before they get away. It was nice seeing you." Then I leave before the person can drag me back in again. When you talk with people in a social setting, most often you want to make a quick hit and get out.

Now, I'll admit that in some circumstances I'm the one who wants to bend somebody's ear and monopolize the conversation—especially if I go somewhere with the specific intent of getting to know one person. In that case, my goal is to be so engaging that the person wants me to stay and talk some more. I'll stay as long as he or she lets me.

Time is valuable. Don't spend too much of it in one place.

Don't blow it

One of the worst things you can do at a social event is to stand around waiting for someone to come to you. After you've talked to everyone you know, get out and introduce yourself to people you don't know. You have to learn to become comfortable with self-introductions if you want to get anywhere in life or business. Say, "Hi, I'm so-and-so. Nice to meet you." They'll shake your hand and you'll catch a short rap. It's simple.

You very rarely see any successful 40- or 50-year-old who doesn't try to meet everyone in the room. It may take 20 or 30 years to learn how important this is, but eventually he or she realizes it. I say, why wait that long? It's most impressive to see young people who know how to enter a room and take charge. That alone says something about the kind of business sense they have and how successful they're ultimately going to be. Older people tell me all the time that they like watching me work a room. "I wish I had done that when I was your age," they say. If a 19- or 20-year-old comes up to me and says, "Mr. Roberts, how are you? I'm so-and-so. It's nice to meet you," I'm thinking, "This is a good kid." I'd find something for that kid to do in my company. It shows a sense of confidence and ambition, two qualities always admired in the business world.

There are a few other "don'ts" you should keep in mind when you head into a room:

- ✓ Don't be rude. When you decide you want to meet somebody, be aggressive and confident, but watch your timing. You can't just butt into somebody's conversation. Wait until this person turns to look for a new conversation—then make your move.

- ✓ Don't arrive fashionably late. If you don't know most of the people at the event, you want to be early so you can watch who arrives and where they sit. You want to get a lay of the land before things start hopping.

✓ Don't ask for autographs from celebrity people you want to build relationships with. Right away, you're saying, "You're much better than I am." You're as good as anybody and you should stand on equal ground.

✓ Don't be too friendly. At an initial meeting, use titles, not first names if the person is older than you. Always say, "Nice to meet you Mr. [or Ms.] Jones." Don't start out saying, "Hi, Bob [or Barbara]." Anyone with a title should also receive this courtesy of being properly addressed: a mayor, a commissioner, a senator, a doctor, a professor, etc. Let them tell you to use their first name.

✓ Don't show signs of insecurity. Power people pick up on weaknesses. You have to act confident and approach on equal footing. That gets you respect.

✓ Don't drink too much. You can make sure that everyone at your table always has a drink, but don't *you* drink. Water is best.

✓ Don't overeat. You can eat like a pig with your friends, but be mannerly and restrained when you're in an environment where you want to make a good impression.

The object of practicing socializing is to get to the point where, when you walk into a room, the room lights up. And all eyes really are on you. That's when you know you're doing it right and it's working.

Critical life lessons

✓ There's no such thing as going out "just for fun." Successful people are always on the lookout for business contacts.

✓ Every time you introduce yourself to a stranger, you open a door of vast possibilities.

✓ It's ironic that shy people are usually mistaken for snotty, conceited people.

✓ Successfully mixing business with pleasure requires that you have a very sincere and warm personality.

✓ Don't let fate stick you in the corner. Size up a room and take charge.

✓ If you slight people you don't know, you risk insulting someone who could have been very important for you to know.

✓ Socially adept people know the rules of the social pecking order: You approach people who are socially or professionally higher on the ladder than you.

✓ Don't let rumors, media, or preconceived judgments keep you from being your charming best with all people. Meet everyone and decide for yourself if you'd like to meet again.

✓ Your handshake can make or break you in the first 30 seconds of a social contact. Shake firmly and look into the person's eyes.

✓ To be a good conversationalist, be well-read.

✓ Rejection is part of the game. Get used to it and keep trying.

✓ Don't run around indiscriminately handing out your business card. It will make you look cheap and easy. Collect other people's cards and use them aggressively to build your business.

✓ If somebody takes up too much of your time, be assertive and move on.

✓ Be aggressive, confident, and secure in all social situations.

Party Hard

I can't think of a single drawback to entertaining for business purposes. It's just the best way to build and sustain your business.

I go out socializing five to six nights every week. My goal is always to have about 12 important people with me—people who can help me, people with whom I can network, and people I want to get to know better. Brokers, investors, media people, and people with connections to athletes are always there. I get to know them; they get to meet each other; they network for their own purposes; we all relax and have some fun. The most productive part of my workday is after working hours.

During the day, I can call up any number of multimillionaires I know. They'll take my call, but they're not going to want to talk to me for too long. They can't loosen up in the middle of their workday. But when we get together socially, they're loose; they're having fun; they're laughing and drinking; they're eating. That's the time I do my business: "Hey, how about investing a million in Worldwide Entertainment and Sports?" The chances of getting a yes when people are "off duty" and relaxed are much higher than if I walked into the middle of their business day and asked the same question.

Business entertaining is so important that it should be written right into your budget—and don't skimp. Some people say, "That Roberts throws around so much money. He's always socializing and taking people out." I'm not bothered by the ridicule. These are envious and short-sighted people who don't understand how socializing and business work together. I probably go to 320 dinners a year, but all I have to do is make one good deal at one of those dinners and it pays for all the others and more. Obviously I make more than one deal a year, so I have no worries about coming out ahead. I've raised more than $12 million this year alone and I know if I hadn't been out there entertaining and networking, this wouldn't have happened.

Meet important people with whom you want to do business after work hours—on weekends, at night, on vacation—any time except during business hours.

Making it happen

It's usually easy to get people to eat good food and hand you the bill. The hard part is getting these people to join you to begin with. Once you've identified someone you'd like to meet after business hours, plan out a strategy. This may be as simple as asking, "How about we get together for dinner tomorrow night?" Sometimes this works, but most often it doesn't. Very successful people are hounded for a piece of their leisure time and are reluctant to give it away to someone they've just met. In this case, you need to be patient and work your way up to a social invitation.

Socializing is the best vehicle you have to get to know somebody with whom you want to do business. The key is to find a way to get him or her to accept your invitation—that's the real trick.

Start out with a very short business call. If you don't really have any business to discuss with this person, make up something— anything to get in touch. Make the call very short, but before ending the conversation, find a reason to send something over to the office. This something may be an article you've seen in the news that you think would be of interest to this person. It could be information about your business that you want to share. Whatever it is, promise to send it and then send it immediately! (See Rule #18 for more details on the value of reliability.)

The next step is to visit face to face. Drop by the office for just a second. You might hand-deliver something or just stick your head in to say hello. Don't stay long—this is a busy person who doesn't have time to chitchat. But make good use of your time by looking around for signs of what the person likes. Look at things like pictures and knickknacks. Find out what the person is interested in. Is it sailing? Baseball? Ping-Pong™? Dogs? These are all pieces of information that can bring you a step closer to a social get-together.

Whatever it is this person likes, use it to open up conversation. Let's say you find out she is into opera. You say, "You like opera! My high school buddy works over at the opera house and he can get us the best seats!" Of course you may have no such connection, but certainly you can find a way to get those tickets. If she says no, and you get a feeling she just doesn't want to go with you, send two tickets and tell her to enjoy herself. After the show, call up and say, "I'm going to be in your area next week. Is it okay if I stop by to say hello?" What's she going to do—not take your call or accept your invitation for lunch? Seven out of 10 people will say yes. Those are pretty good odds.

Even when I had no money, I still found ways to give people the things that would help me get close to them. I remember when I wanted Emanuel Steward to be my mentor. (Steward is a boxing trainer who has worked with the greats, including Hearns, Holyfield, Lennox Lewis, and now Shannon Briggs.) He told me he wanted to see the Broadway show *Dream Girls,* so I told him I had connections and could get him these tough-to-find tickets. My only "connection" was a local ticket broker, but I got them, and suddenly Emanual thought I was somebody special.

Some people worry they'll be annoying if they call, and stop by to visit, and send little gifts. I say, "What's the option?" I'd rather be annoying and have a chance, than not be annoying and have no chance. The worst thing people can do is ignore you or tell you to get lost. If the option is not getting what you want, what's the risk? I'll go with annoying, even if it gives me only a 10-percent chance.

Pick the place

When you think you've gotten to know a person well enough to begin socializing, you have to decide where to go. Home entertaining is good if you have a nice home where a person can be relaxed and at ease, but I think it's harder to keep a person entertained at home unless you're having a big party with lots of people. I like to entertain in restaurants and clubs. There the environment is upbeat; I know everybody likes to eat, and I can invite several people at one time. I also like it because this kind of invitation is easy to extend: "What's your favorite food? Oh! I know the greatest Italian restaurant you have to try. I'm sure you'll love it. How's Tuesday night?" How can anyone turn down an invitation like that?

Another way of socializing for profit is to go wherever you think the other person would like to go. If he likes to go drinking, you may have to suck it up and go out with him. If she likes golfing, go hit some balls at the driving range. If he likes baseball, rent a batting cage for him. If she likes fishing, head for the high seas with a hired boat and captain. Find out what people like and (whether you like it or not) do it with them.

When I was getting to know Morty Davis (who built the dynasty D.H. Blair Investment Banking Corp., and who ended up being the key investment broker who helped me take my first company public), he invited me to Sabbath dinner at his house with his daughter and son-in-law. Maybe this wasn't something I'd suggest myself, but you can bet I was there in a flash. This kind of socializing led to my African safari and my trip to China with Morty later on.

Wherever you go, remember that the first goal is to relax and socialize. Don't make it obvious that it is no more than a business meeting in a different environment. Don't ever go into a restaurant with your briefcase in hand or pull out your pad and pen at the table. This makes people tense. Successful people are always on guard against people who want something out of them. Everywhere they turn, somebody has a hand out. The plan is to get together and have some fun—that's how you eventually get things done.

Socializing will eventually lead to business gains, if you don't try too hard to begin with. Pick places where you can relax, have fun, and get to know people.

Moving on

So now you've made contact on the phone, you've sent something nice, you've arranged a personal meeting at the office and you've extended an invitation to meet socially. If the person still resists, you have to decide if it's time to move on or keep trying. Some people are just not interested—no point in spinning your wheels. Maybe this person is already in tight with somebody else in your business. You don't want to spend a lot of time and energy cultivating a relationship with somebody who can't be penetrated. If you do these steps and you get a gut feeling that the person just isn't going to respond, try the next person on your list. Not everybody loves me; I just move on. If you make a hit with three out of 10 of your targets, you're doing pretty well.

On the other hand, some people just take longer than others. If you are trying to get close to someone who you feel is vital to your success in the business, don't be too quick to give up just because they don't want to know your name. I remember when I wanted to get to know Cedric Kushner. He was my competitor in the boxing field and he wouldn't even give me the time of day. But I knew if he just got to know me and find out the kind of agent I was, we could put some great events together. I had to keep being friendly every time I saw him at boxing events. I'd always wave, go over to shake hands, send him follow-up information. I had to make all the attempts at personal contact because he wasn't interested in knowing me. Finally, after about 10 years, we went out to dinner a few times and that did the trick. Getting people in a social environment can break down even the toughest resistance.

There may be people out there who don't want to be entertained; you've got to be able to read that and just be all business during business hours. But you can assume that most people like to be entertained.

Kick back and open up

When the person with whom you want to socialize says yes to your invitation, your next goal is to get to know each other. Don't blow the whole point of meeting socially by cutting short your small talk to get right to business. If the people you're trying to get to know better are very successful, you're no more than one of that crowd of people lining up around the block if you don't first get the person to relax and get to know you before you ask for something. Ironically, it's often the most successful people who have no one to talk to. Everybody is always after them for business favors, not their companionship. Take your time, let these people relax and get to know and like you before you move to business matters.

When you socialize, make the most of your time by keeping these tips in mind:

- ✓ Don't act like a stuffed shirt—have a few laughs.

- ✓ Don't be in awe just because this is a big fish. You are just as smart and just as good a human being as the other person.

- ✓ Don't get tense and say stupid things. Remember, you're here for fun, so just be yourself.

- ✓ Be an attentive host. Make sure their glass is always full. Make sure they know everybody else. Make sure they feel comfortable and relaxed.

- ✓ Be a good conversationalist. People usually think you're a great conversationalist if you listen to them talk about themselves. Plan to ask simple questions that keep the conversation focused on them: "Did you enjoy your dinner?" "Do you have any kids? Tell me about them."

Personal information is the gauge I use to measure when I'm getting close to someone. You know you've got someone when you start hearing personal stuff. As soon as I hear things like, "Oh, my marriage is torture," or "I went to college but I really didn't know what I wanted to do," or "Let me tell you about my first big deal," I always know I'm in with the guy. It's the stuff a person wouldn't tell you on a cold call.

A good conversationalist is really a good listener.
Steer the conversation away from yourself by getting the
person to open up and tell you his or her life story.

Pace yourself

There are only 24 hours in a day. I can't socialize too much just for the fun of it. Let's be honest: If I'm going to invest a lot of time and money in people, I'm going to do it with an eye toward doing business with them. But that doesn't mean I'm anxious to talk business at our first dinner before the meal is served. I'm a young guy and I look at everything long term. When I first invite people to dinner, I don't ask them for anything. It can take a couple of months or a year or two to really get to know some people and feel confident that they want to help me. I can tell really fast if a person is a snob and not worth my time, but once I decide someone is a good person and has promising potential as a business contact, I'm happy to give that person my time and attention.

When you've socialized with people for a long time, very often you'll find they don't really buy into your business, but into *you*. That's why you have to give them time to get to know you. About a year ago, I met a young guy who was a successful real estate developer with lots of money. But I could tell he was conservative and wouldn't be excited about investing in a sports management company. I started seeing him socially and found out that when he loosens up, he really enjoys a good night out. I saw that he was getting a real kick from the excitement of going to nightclubs and meeting beautiful women. Soon he was investing heavily in Worldwide Entertainment and Sports. Actually, he was investing in *me*; this person got to know me and understood my drive for success. He knew I wouldn't let him down.

Don't hurry the getting-to-know-you process. Friendships take time to develop. Business relationships are no different.

Don't drop the ball

It's great to entertain, but you've got to stay in touch afterward if you want anything to happen. I make at least a hundred keeping-in-touch calls a day. I pick up the phone and just give a quick, "Hello, it was good seeing you. We'll get together again real soon." Boom, done, follow-up. I've never been big on writing notes, but it's a good idea if you like to do it. I think it's nice of people to take the time to write something down and send it out. If the get-together was something special, I might follow up with a gift—something such as a fruit basket or flowers. When I first met Steve Hamilton (one of the biggest stockbrokers in the world with Ladenburg Thalmann & Co.), Joe Glodek (with William Scott, the company who took me public), and Todd Roberti (owner of the brokerage firm LT Lawrence), I sent each one a boxing glove signed by Ray Mercer or Shannon Briggs. Whatever it is, you have to do something to get back in touch with people you've socialized with.

Sometimes the follow-up is more than a quick hello. If I leave someone feeling really confident that he or she is ready to do business, I'm not going to just sit around and hope. I'll call the next day or the day after and say, "I'm going to be in your area today. I could stop by with the contracts if that's convenient for you," or whatever gets you in the door with the contract. Don't be bashful about asking for things. If you don't ask, you won't get. There's no point in doing all that entertaining if you're not going to follow it up.

When you're ready to move from socializing to business, you've got to be the aggressor and assume nothing's going to happen unless you initiate it.

Sometimes I'll socialize and keep in touch with somebody for years even though there's nothing happening business-wise at the moment. If I know this person is sharp and bound to be into good things somewhere down the line, I want to be the first in line to reap the benefits. A guy like that, for example, is Lou Falcigno. I met Lou when I was 19 years old. At that time, he was the biggest distributor of closed-circuit TV events in the country. (Before pay-per-view, people used to watch the big fights in movie theaters or sports arenas on closed circuit TV. Ali, Frazier, Cooney, Holmes, Sugar Ray Leonard, Thomas Hearns, Roberto Duran, and Hagler all had boxing events shown on closed-circuit TV.) Lou sold me a couple of locations for boxing matches and I promoted the events so well, I used to make more money on one location than most people would make on 50. We made a lot of money together and built a great relationship. But then the pay-per-view business made the closed-circuit industry obsolete. Some people might look at that and figure Lou Falcigno was no longer a big player—no point in socializing with him anymore. But I knew Lou was successful in closed-circuit because he was a very smart businessman, and I knew he'd be versatile enough to figure out what the next hot thing would be and become very successful again. I wasn't going to turn my back on this guy; I wanted to be there when he rose to the top again. We kept in touch for 20 years, and sure enough, we just recently made another great deal together: I introduced him to the people at D.H. Blair who helped us both buy a record company that ended up going public and then was bought out by TCI Music.

The question is: When the deal is done, is it time to move on to somebody else? I think it depends on the person. There's no way you can keep a good relationship going with every person you meet and do business with. But if the person is as smart and savvy and ambitious as Lou Falcigno, then you can be sure there's always going to be another good deal down the road that you'll want to be in on. In that case, I'd stay in touch.

After you sign

Business entertaining isn't just to land accounts, it's to keep them, too. In 1997, we wanted to sign basketball player Bobby Jackson out of Minnesota. We got to know him; we pampered him; we did everything. Finally, he signed (and was picked in the first round of the NBA draft). With his contract secure, we could have been quick to move on to the next hot athlete—especially with a basketball rookie, because we don't make money on NBA guys until they become free agents. (Rookies are slotted in the NBA for a given salary.) But that's not how we work. It just so happened that Bobby's birthday was the day after the basketball draft, so we threw him the biggest party he ever saw. We invited his friends and family, and had cake, and champagne, and everything—it was a $5,000-bash!

You can't schmooze people to get their account or investment and then stop calling as soon as you get it. First off, it's bad business, low class, and rude. But also these are the people who can help you build your business. Now you should invite them to come with you when you're recruiting new people. If they're satisfied with your work, they're your best advertisement. Let them tell everyone else at the party how great you are, and at the same time let them continue to enjoy the same hospitality and attention you gave them when you were "courting."

Business socializing isn't something you do when you have some downtime. It's what you do constantly to keep your business alive and thriving.

Critical life lessons

✓ If you're willing to put money into having fun, it will come back to you in profits.

✓ You have to patiently strategize how to work your way into the good graces of people with whom you want to socialize for business purposes—it rarely just happens by accident.

✓ When you're planning social activities, think about what the other person likes—even if you hate it.

✓ Persistently pursue what you want, but be smart enough to know when you've hit a dead end.

✓ Life is not all work and business. Kick back and enjoy yourself with the right people and watch the business contacts fall into place.

✓ Good conversationalists don't necessarily know how to tell captivating stories. They know how to get other people to tell stories.

✓ Always assume nothing profitable will come of a good time unless you aggressively follow up with smart business moves.

✓ The party isn't over after you close the deal. Be smart and keep in touch socially with all people who are important to your business.

Keep Your Enemies Close

*When you're tempted to blow a gasket, you've got to stop and
think. It might make you feel good to yell and shout obscenities.
But being successful is all about thinking about consequences.
Will you get exactly what you want with this kind of outburst?
Or will you get it by letting the other person think you're still
on friendly terms?*

It's a fact of life: We all have enemies. The key is to decide how
you're going to deal with them. How you treat your enemies will determine if the evil in others brings you down to their level where you
both lose, or if you rise above them and let them unwittingly be the
support that pushes you closer to your goal.

The long road to justice

I learned about dealing with my enemies very early in my business life, and the lessons learned from one particular experience still
guide many of the things I do today. It all started because I wanted to
get to know Bob Arum (who, along with Don King, is the biggest promoter in boxing history). From the second I decided to manage boxers,
I knew he was somebody to get close to. To wrangle an introduction, I
went through one of his entourage. When I was 22 years old and had
just finished my successful fights in Plainfield, N.J., he came to me
and asked if I'd like to be a partner in the distribution and production
of closed-circuit TV events. "You put the money up," he said, "and I'll
get you the rights to certain areas." So we became partners and we
both made a lot of money on the arrangement. As a bonus, I knew all
along that he was saying great things about me to Bob Arum and
that would be my entrée into a close relationship.

One day, someone in Arum's entourage came to me and said, "Listen, do you want to buy into Donald Curry?" At that time, Donald Curry was a promising fighter with 13 wins out of 13 fights who had the potential to be the next great fighter. But with only 13 fights, nothing was for sure. I was told I could buy into this fighter for $27,500 and own four percentage points of him until I made my money back; then we'd split 2 percent each. Hey, if the fighter hit for $10 million, 2 percent would be $200,000 for me. That was a fortune to me at the time. I sold my car (again), and just about everything else I had in the world and bought into this deal. My lawyer, Norman Fishbein (a tough, Newark, N.J., lawyer), drew up a simple, clear-cut contract and I owned a piece of another fighter.

Curry's next fight was with Marlin Starling (who went on to have an exciting career). The day of the fight, Curry was four pounds overweight—he spent the day fasting and sitting in the sauna. Things didn't look so good. He ended up winning the fight on a split decision by the skin of his teeth. This was nerve-wracking! But he went on to win his next five fights, and I was making my money back. People were saying he was the next superstar, the next Sugar Ray, the next Marvin Hagler. I just wanted him to win the next fight in Monaco. Here I would get my first taste of real profit if Curry beat Nino LaRocca (who was 44 and 0). If he won that match, we knew he would go on to fight for $5- or $10 million.

About two weeks before we were set to leave for France, my partner called me down to Atlantic City. He told me, "You weren't supposed to tell anybody about this deal. But your friend Bobby Davimos knows all about it and he told Donald that you're involved. Now Donald is mad and I've got to take back those points I offered you." What?? I had paid for this share of Curry's wins and I had a signed contract agreeing to the deal. There was no way Bobby had interfered with my business, and even if he had, there was no way Curry would care. Was this guy nuts? What was I supposed to do next?

Since I had signed the contract, Norman Fishbein had died. If he had still been around, there was no way I would have been bumped out of that contract. But as things stood, I knew there was no way I was ever going to get anything out of a Curry fight again. At that point, I figured I had two options: 1) I could go crazy. I could throw a fit, cursing, and threatening, and the whole bit. (Socking him in the face was out because he was much bigger than me.) Or 2) I could stay calm and act like it didn't bother me, while I planned to get payback.

Every part of me was screaming for option number one. I wanted to tell him off and then tell everybody I knew what a crook he was. But I had to remember that this was the person who had the connection to Bob Arum. What would I accomplish (besides a great sense of personal relief) if I broke all ties with him? How would it benefit me to lose contact with Bob Arum because of this jerk? It's not smart to go to war with powerful people. So I went with option number two and walked out of the room saying, "I'm sure you'll take care of me one of these days."

I was steamed. I had my tickets all set for my trip to Monaco. I was ready to finally cash in. And here I was out in the cold. Even giving him the benefit of the doubt, if things had happened as he said, no good person would ever propose a deal like that to a young kid, let him sell everything to buy in, and then let him be thrown aside just when the deal was about to pay off. You just don't do that. Besides, I didn't believe his motives were so innocent. So I rolled up my sleeves to get to the bottom of what had happened. The first thing I did was call Bobby Davimos to verify that he hadn't talked to Curry. He hadn't. Then I jumped on a plane and went to see Curry in Texas to find out if he objected to my owning two percentage points. He didn't. Now I knew that my partner had taken my points just to screw me out of what was rightfully and legally mine. Even though I was devastated, I kept remembering an old saying: "Keep your friends close, but keep your enemies closer." He had just become my enemy, and I wanted to keep him close.

First, I hired a lawyer to sue for my percentage points, just to cover myself in case Curry really did make it to the top. (This was a terrific learning experience: At a very young age I learned everything about litigation, depositions, interrogatories, etc.) But I kept in touch with this guy. I told him the suit was just business, nothing personal. I told him my dad had hired this lawyer, but I was trying to quash the whole thing. I told him I knew the mess was Bobby Davimos's fault and that I hoped we could still do business. I'm sure he was thinking, "Boy, this kid really is a schmuck. I probably could have gotten another hundred grand out of him." But I was just waiting for the right time to show who the real schmuck was. I made sure we kept a good dialogue going. He had no idea I was out to get him.

The whole key to keeping your enemies close is a deep discipline that allows you to act like buddies with people who you know will burn you without a second thought.

I got my first piece of justice sooner than I thought I would. First off, I didn't really lose that much money. Curry started losing as soon as I stepped out of his career. (This was a pattern that would recur again and again when fighters like Ray Mercer and Charles Murray left my management.) Curry became one of the biggest disappointments in boxing history. Much of this was caused by the fact that he lost focus because of mismanagement.

I continued my relationship with my now ex-partner and things worked out just like I thought they would. I continued my work with him on the closed-circuit territories and he brought me in close contact with Bob Arum who became one of my mentors. Sure, I had to swallow my pride. I had to play it meek. (I'd even do favors for him when he asked me!) But the whole time, I kept myself focused on justice. I did such a good job at keeping up the charade that he approached *me* about managing Olympic boxers. Bingo! This sounded like payback time.

I finally met Bob Arum through introductions by this guy. I got to spend time with him, study his moves, learn about his organization, travel overseas, and socialize with him. My plan was working beautifully. In 1988, I went with Arum to Arizona to talk to the coaches of the Olympic boxing team. We agreed that after the Olympic matches, Arum would be the boxers' promoter and I would pick three to manage. I chose the cream of the crop: Ray Mercer (who won the gold medal), Charles Murray, and Al Cole. This was my first big-time situation that eventually led to Triple Threat Enterprises. Never in a million years would all of this have happened if I hadn't kept my enemy close. I wouldn't have been able to get these big-name boxers, start my company, and then go public if I had done what I really wanted to do after my points were taken away.

I waited five years for my patience to pay off. It was especially sweet when Triple Threat went public. If this guy hadn't burned me and had still been working with me, I would have given him so much stock in Triple Threat Enterprises (which five years later went up to $125!) that he would have been a multimillionaire. But I didn't give him one share. And with my new company, Worldwide Entertainment and Sports, I would have given him more stock on which to make millions. Instead, he left Arum to manage Curry full-time and never got back into anything big again. His life today is nothing compared to what it could have been if he had been straight with me—and he knows it.

The best way to get even with an enemy is to make him your friend, and then profit from the relationship. This takes some cunning and lots of patience, but it's the best revenge on earth.

Watch your back

If somebody bad-mouths me and I find out about it, it's no problem—I pretend I didn't hear it. But my relationship with that person changes immediately. That person drops down into the basement of my hierarchy of relationships, and I don't forget it. That person will never again benefit through a relationship with me. And if the talk was really malicious, I will get even, but the person won't even know what happened. I've gotten justice from people who, to this day, probably don't even know it was me who took them down. I know this sounds awful, but I guess because I'm so willing to give my best to other people, I feel it hard when I get stabbed in the back. I don't usually get justice through any kind of public scene or angry outburst. I'll use business dealings to get even when it's necessary.

Let me give you a perfect example of what I mean. I used to be very friendly with a ticket broker, and I had a long-standing friend working for me. They both had access to all my key people. Back in the early 90s they were running a major show in South Mountain Arena in New Jersey for me. This was really big: Ray Mercer, Charles Murray, and Al Cole—the whole Triple Threat—were on the card. George Foreman was giving an exhibition fight at that event, too, to begin his comeback. And on top of that, Tommy Morrison was fighting and he was also staring in a *Rocky* movie, so Sylvester Stallone and Burt Young were going to work his corner with all the cameras filming the movie right at the event. All this in one night! Tickets started flying like crazy. There wasn't even going to be standing room outside.

I was happy to have these two guys run this event because I was really busy at that time getting ready to take the company public. I was running around meeting with all kinds of people, borrowing from here to pay over there. If you didn't know better, or have great faith in me, you'd think I was about to bury myself in debt and overextension.

Somewhere these guys got the idea that I was in a weak position and ripe for a takeover. They figured I was going to crash and they were setting themselves up to step into my shoes.

Their first move was to keep me in the dark about what was happening with this big event. They weren't telling me how many tickets were sold; they weren't giving me tickets for my big clients and investors; they weren't even returning my phone calls. About one month before the fight, I realized I had a *big* problem: They told people who were close to me that I was going broke, that I was overextended, that I had dug myself into a hole, and that they were going to take over. Of course I heard all of this.

I'm sure most people would have ripped the tickets right out of their hands and shown them the door. But this was too big of a show to screw up in anger. What should I do? If I got really mad and took back control and threw them out, I'd have a mess on my hands, because I had been busy enough to let these guys have all the tickets, all the money, and all the cards. If I took back control at that point, how would I explain to my investors, the press, and the TV executives the chaos that would result? I wouldn't know who had tickets and who didn't. I couldn't issue new tickets and have people showing up with old ones and have two people in one seat. This was a high-profile event that could easily turn into a nightmare. I would have to wait to fix the situation. My reputation was on the line.

I decided to let them both play big-shots for four weeks. I played real innocent and dumb. If they thought I was weak, I was going to play weak. That made them work even harder to make this one of the best events because they thought they would directly reap the benefits when they took over. I also didn't want to let on that I knew anything was wrong, because they were taking in all the money. I knew they were going to rob me for about $20,000, but I hoped to cut it at that and at least break even. The loss of this money was far less than what it would have cost me if the whole event fell apart. That was another reason that I had to play it very cool. I was courting investors to go public, and my name was on the line with this event. Yeah, these guys took over the fight, but my name was still on the marquee outside. I was willing to pay that price to have things run smoothly.

The night of the fight, my patience paid off. The place was packed with about 4,200 people. Hundreds more were outside waiting for Stallone, Mercer, Foreman, and Morrison. It was a fabulous night. It couldn't have been better. I was the king. People were congratulating me all night. My name blanketed the press the next day. And I received congratulatory calls from the governor on down telling me that I had put together an event that gave the people just what they wanted. This event was a great boost for my reputation.

The next day, I walked into the office and sat down with the two guys who put on the show. Still playing my routine, I said, "Let's sit down and see what happened last night." The three of us went over the receipts and congratulated each other. Then, the minute I had the cash in my hands and was sure I hadn't lost too much, I told them both I knew exactly what was going on. I told them that greed had just ruined their careers and that their lack of loyalty was going to cost them big—they were out. I knew I'd never need these guys again for anything (if I did I'd be in big trouble anyway). I wasn't worried about burning any bridges here. I wanted nothing to do with them for anything. I kept them real close until I didn't need them anymore. (Although I admit, for sentimental reasons, I did give my friend another shot at working for me later on.)

Rather than go to war with people who burn me, I keep them close so I can learn what they're doing and what they're thinking. This way, I catch them by surprise just when they think things are going their way. That's how they learn that loyalty and honesty are important character traits.

Watch your mouth

My mentor Morty Davis used to tell me to always say good things about everybody so what you say can never come back to haunt you. That's a good philosophy to live by—but not always easy to do. When someone has treated you badly, there's a strong temptation to let the world know what he did to you. But there's nothing to gain in doing that. You're more likely to get what you want in life if you keep your mouth shut when you're tempted to blast somebody's reputation. I'm not saying that I don't make that person regret crossing me. As I've said, I have been known to blow a deal or two for people who've hurt me, but I wouldn't say bad things about them in public. (I admit that in this book I have bad-mouthed a few people who have burned me in the past. I've thought long and hard about doing this and have decided that these are people I never want in my life again. The purpose of avoiding bad-mouthing is to make sure you don't burn any bridges. In a few cases, I am intentionally striking the match.)

I'm always amazed when I meet someone and we start talking about people we know and the person says, "Oh, I know him. What an idiot." How can somebody I just met say that to me? The person we're talking about might be my best friend. When any name comes up in conversation of someone I like a lot, I'll go on and on building that person up. I'll say, "What a great person! He's [she's] the best. There's nobody like so-and-so." But if I don't like the person because I think he or she is unscrupulous, or dishonest, or unloyal, or whatever, I'll always simply say, "He's [she's] a nice person." That's all. It keeps me out of trouble. What good is it going to do me to say a person's a jerk to somebody who knows the person? Naturally, he'll go back and say, "You should hear what Marc Roberts said about you." Of course, I have close friends who I talk openly with and show my true feelings. But even then I have to be sure what I say is kept private. If I'm thinking about trusting somebody, sometimes I'll test them a few times before I really open up. I'll tell them some kind of dirt about a mutual friend. Then I'll call that friend and say, "Listen, I just said some negative stuff about you to so-and-so. Let me know if it gets back to you." It's important to know who you can trust when you're keeping your enemies close.

There's nothing to gain and everything to lose when you bad-mouth somebody.

Leave room for mistakes

I discovered another reason to keep my enemies close quite by accident. Some people with whom I was really angry, but who I kept close anyway, turned out to be not so bad, and because I didn't make a big scene about what they did, we ended up being good business associates and/or friends down the line. I first learned the value of keeping quiet about adversaries back in 7th grade when a guy named Terry Rucker (who went to a rival school) started dating the girl I was after. I hated Terry for a couple of years but I never made a scene or bad-mouthed him. I don't know exactly how it happened but we ended up being friends—in fact I was the best man at his wedding! To this day, he is a friend I count on and with whom I keep in constant touch.

I remembered this lesson when I first met both Dino Duva and Cedric Kushner (both big fight promoters). They definitely didn't like me. I was a new kid trying to work my way into the business and they stayed away from me. I couldn't even get a nod hello when we passed in the hall. But I didn't make any kind of confrontation out of the situation. As I grew in reputation over the years and we spent more time together and did more events together, we all found out that we worked well together. Now somebody else might not want anything to do with people who wouldn't help an inexperienced newcomer, but who suddenly get buddy-buddy when he raises millions of dollars, has hot fighters, and is getting great publicity. I didn't take that attitude. My plan was to be patient with these guys and prove myself, and that's exactly what happened.

There will be lots of times when you don't hit it off right away with somebody, but don't do something stupid that will close the door on future deals. Be patient.

There was a time when I almost broke off a relationship because I misjudged someone. If I hadn't kept this person close when I thought he was an enemy, I would never have found out the truth and made a good friend at the same time. It was when I had my major trouble with Jack Dell. (You'll remember, he's the investor who introduced me to the underwriter who took my company public, became my partner in Triple Threat, and then took the company and the fighters out from under me.) I hired Tom Gallagher as my lawyer to help me out of this bind. He did a good job; I came out of the deal happy and I figured everything was over. Then two months later, I found out that Gallagher was working for Jack Dell. Wait a minute! He just negotiated my deal with Jack Dell and now he was the general counsel for all of Triple Threat—the company that I founded and just got screwed out of! Some people might have jumped right on that and sued Gallagher for conflict of interest, but I decided to play it cool until I could find out what had happened. I was happy with the deal Gallagher got me, but now I was thinking maybe I could have gotten much more.

I had to figure that one of two things had happened: Either 1) Dell got a hold of Gallagher and said something like, "Make sure I come out okay on this case with Roberts and I'll make you millions, or 2) Gallagher was a very ethical and talented lawyer, and when Jack Dell saw that he was a sharp, young guy, he wanted Gallagher on his side. I wasn't ready to jump to conclusions on either side.

I kept in touch with Gallagher. We talked a lot. He always let me know what was going on with "my" boxers. Finally, over time, I became convinced that what happened was probably number two: He was a damned good lawyer who Jack Dell wanted on his side. If I hadn't given myself the time and space to realize this, I would have cut myself off from a good and honest person. I would have made a scene and falsely accused him of terrible things. I probably would have demanded a commission, because Triple Threat became his biggest client, paying him a lot of money every year, besides what he was making off of the Triple Threat stock he owned, which had jumped to $125. Maybe I even would have sued him in court. Where would all this have gotten me?

There's even more to this story: Several years later, I went in to pitch Worldwide to Steve Hamilton at Ladenburg Thalmann & Co. (Steve is a one-man powerhouse and one of the most talented brokers in the world.) I expected to be rejected because I knew he didn't listen to people representing stocks that traded below $10 (which mine did). But when he heard me mention Triple Threat, he opened right up. It turned out that Steve started out at F.N. Wolf (my underwriter) and made a lot of money off Triple Threat and he remembered the deal fondly. "Do you know Tom Gallagher?" he asked. "Sure," I said. "We're buddies." Steve lit up. It seemed he knew Tom back when they were both involved with F.N. Wolf. "Tom's the greatest guy!" he went on. "Could you have him call me? I'd love to see him again. And—sure, sure, I'll get behind you."

Just imagine how that meeting would have gone if I had taken the other road with Gallagher. What would I now be saying to Steve Hamilton who could take my new company to a higher level? But because I was willing to lay low and get at the truth, Gallagher was now in my corner. I think he knew that I could have made a scene without understanding the facts and he appreciated my attitude.

That night I called Gallagher and told him about my conversation with Steve Hamilton. "Steve would love to hear from you," I said. So Tom called Steve, and then the conversation turned to me. Glowing testimonials coming from Tom Gallagher, who Steve respected and admired, were like the word of God. Two days later, Hamilton got involved with the stock and he himself bought a couple of hundred thousand shares of the stock. This was my payback for keeping Tom Gallagher close when I thought he might have been my enemy. Without Tom's recommendation, Steve Hamilton wouldn't have remembered my name the next day.

If you keep people close, even when you suspect they're unscrupulous,
you can watch and listen and learn the truth.

Prove people wrong

This same theory also works the other way around. There will be times when people just don't like you—for whatever reason. If you treat them like dirt because you're not on the top of their list, then you give them a reason not to like you. Don't let your ego get in the way of keeping your enemies close. If there's someone you want on your side but that person wants nothing to do with you, don't get angry; get friendly. Always be pleasant and kind. Keep in touch. Most people will eventually come around.

Sports columnist Jerry Izenberg tells me that there are one or two writers in the sports business who do not like me. They don't like me because they don't trust boxing managers to begin with. They see me out there pushing hard and they automatically label me as no good. Then they begin checking into my business. They ask around to find some dirt. They talk to the boxers and trainers. They never find anything and they start to notice that I'm always good to them, that I'm true to my word, that I treat my athletes well. I let my record speak for me and I usually come out on top. But if I were to curse out these writers for jumping to conclusions—I would prove them right and I would lose in the end.

Keeping your enemies close may be the hardest thing you do in your career. It takes a personal discipline to stay calm. It takes integrity to keep your mouth shut. It takes a clear view of what you want to happen through this relationship in the future. But despite the difficulties, it's a tactic that always pays off in the end.

Critical life lessons

✓ You have to think about the consequences of anger before you let people know what you think of them.

✓ Enemies are a fact of life. It's what you do with your enemies that affects the quality of your life.

✓ When your gut is screaming for you to speak your mind, that's when you should keep your mouth shut.

✓ Your mother was right: If you can't say something nice, don't say anything at all.

✓ The only way you can keep in touch with what people are thinking and doing is by keeping them close. Once you turn away from them, you're in the dark.

✓ We all make mistakes in character judgments. Keeping people close, even when their character is suspect, is the best way to arrive at the truth.

✓ Don't rely on others to supply you with character references. Find out for yourself.

✓ The fastest way to confirm rumors that you're no good is to respond with anger. That's proof enough for some people.

✓ Think for 10 seconds before opening your mouth in anger.

Stand Out from the Crowd

---

*If my friends were asked to pick one word to describe me, they'd
probably all pick "unique." Whatever the norm is, I do the opposite.
Right from the start, this was how it had to be. The norm for a nice
Jewish boy like me was to get a college degree and then go to
graduate school. People thought I was out of my mind when I quit
school, but I have always done what I felt in my heart was best,
whether it was popular or not.*

I don't think it's necessary to hire a brass band or wear bizarre
outfits to stand out from the crowd. I think the ability to be perceived
as unique and creative comes from the everyday attitude and business practices you adapt as your signature.

Polish your people skills

If you want to stand out from the crowd, you've got to polish your
people skills. These are the tactics and strategies you use to network,
to socialize, to meet successful people. Everybody does these things—
it's up to you to find a way that sets you apart from "everybody."

Want to be really different? Instead of trying to make yourself look
good, put your energy into making other people feel good. Give compliments, encouragement, and attention to everybody around you—
make people feel special. In the business world, this is not the norm.
Many businesspeople are either too standoffish or too self-absorbed to
make the effort to separate themselves from the crowd by reaching
out to the crowd.

Because everybody is "too busy" to call people just to say hello, or
to socialize just for fun, or to send follow-up notes and gifts, you can
immediately set yourself apart by doing these things. This isn't really

hard to do. It can be something as simple as sending birthday or anniversary cards. Everybody sends a greeting during the winter holidays—that's the norm. Be different and let people know you think of them on their special days. This will work best if you start a computer address book that includes people's home and business numbers and addresses, the names of spouses, girlfriends or boyfriends, birthdays, anniversaries, hobbies, everything. This database will grow through the years and help you stay in touch with everyone who can help build your career through each stage.

It's pretty easy to get into the habit of making the people you know feel special. It gets a little harder when you take this idea to the next level and do the same for people you don't know. But it's usually worth the effort. That's why I treat everyone right—everyone. I do this because the old cliché is absolutely true: You never know who you're talking to. You never know where they'll end up, who they know, and how they can help you.

If I meet someone I know absolutely nothing about, I treat that person like a king. I know there are lots of very wealthy and successful people out there who don't advertise their position because they don't want people hanging on them for favors, or for security reasons, or simply because they're private people. They want to see how people treat them as people, not as business contacts. Of course they love it when they're treated with respect and kindness just for themselves, not their money and power. This is a people skill that can pay off big in the long run. On the other hand, if I find out the person I've been treating like a king is really just starting out, I'll try to figure out how I can help him in his career. If I can turn his life around, he'll remember that. Giving away a few minutes of kindness and consideration is never a waste.

To be truly unique, you should be nice to *everybody*—bellhops, secretaries, mail carriers, waiters, and so on. I make sure I'm nice even to the young kids who come up to me thinking I'm something special. Hey, when they make it into their own, say one or even 15 years from now, I'll still be young and they'll remember that I was good to them. I'm sure somehow I'll benefit from this small kindness. I remember the people who treated me with respect when I was a kid, like my mentor, Harvey Silverman. I'll always be indebted to him.

*If you treat everybody you meet like they're somebody important,
you'll prove you're a different breed of businessperson and you'll
definitely reap the benefits down the road, because people remember
even the smallest kindness.*

Admit what you don't know

Instead of trying to hide the fact that I don't have all the answers, I use that as a strength to get to know important people. I'm a young guy learning the ropes and I look for people who can help me. I tell people, "You're the best. I want to learn from you." I've found that there are a lot of successful people out there who are very willing to help. When I was putting together the deal to take my company public, I knew nothing about the stock market. I never even owned a stock before. There were plenty of people who helped me learn about the law, and contracts, and IPOs and so on. I would have been a fool to insist I knew it all—I knew nothing!

Too many people struggle longer than they need to on their journey to the top because they think it's important to give the impression that they know it all. They think it's a sign of weakness to admit that they have a lot to learn. I wouldn't admit ignorance to somebody I'm trying to close a deal with, but when I'm putting the deal together, I sure am open to all the help I can get from experienced, seasoned, successful people.

Take risks with money

If you want to be different, you have to stick your neck out financially. There's no way around it—it costs money to stand out from the crowd. Too many people figure they'll invest in advertising when they have the money to do so. Well, how are they going to make it big if nobody knows they're out there? I was spending big money on promotions when I was broke because I knew it was important to look like I was the biggest thing to hit my industry. People thought I was a millionaire way before I actually was one. This perception helped me reach that goal. Important and influential people would look at me as a young kid, thinking I had so much money and figure I must really be a smart guy. Then they wanted to get to know me and do business with me. My plan worked beautifully, but it put me in debt up to my ears. Not only was I not worth a million at that time, I wasn't worth a dime. I figure if your goal is to be Joe Average and live a nice, comfortable life of no special significance, then you can go with the naysayers who tell you, "Never spend more than you have." But if your goal is to become a millionaire, you're going to have to take a few financial risks to make it happen.

You'll open up more doors if you take the risk to invest in yourself and your image than if you look like the rest of the gang struggling to reach the top. Perception is everything.

Be relentless

The majority of people give up too easily. If you want to be different, refuse to take no for an answer. You'll find in business that true persistence, perseverance, and determination are rare commodities. Anyone who has these traits is automatically unique. It's an old cliché that says, "A winner never quits and a quitter never wins," and everybody agrees—but few live by it. I do! That very quote sits under my high school yearbook picture. I won't quit. I won't give up. I'll wear people down and make them sick of me but I won't give up.

Drawing on an ancient Chinese proverb, Harry S Truman said in his memoirs that being president "is like riding a tiger. A man has to keep on riding or be swallowed." Life is like that, too, making perseverance crucial to success.

Be ethical

I believe that good wins out in the end—in this I think I'm different. An awful lot of people cheat and steal their way to big money. But from what I see, this kind of success is short term because life has a way of coming down on people who take ethical shortcuts. This belief is what keeps me in line. If I didn't believe there was a morality issue to consider, I'd probably be out there with all the rest not caring who I left wounded in my dust. But that's not the way I work. I believe that God will eventually get me if I take too many moral shortcuts, and He'll reward me if I don't. So I've separated myself from leagues of people in my business simply by being ethical.

In my business, people either love you or they hate you, so there are certainly people who hate me. But nobody will ever say I was unethical or went back on my word. I've built a reputation for honesty over the years that has become my legacy. People say, "If you deal with Marc Roberts, he'll give you a straight answer." "If Marc Roberts says he'll deliver, he will." Right away, I'm unique. Sometimes I might be in a situation where I can't make everybody happy; when I give a fight to one promoter, another promoter will say I screwed him. Stuff like that I can't avoid, but nobody will ever say that I was unethical about it.

I'm not saying that being ethical will always get you a pat on the back; sometimes no one but you knows the truth. But in the end, does anything else matter? After the Briggs–Foreman fight, for example, lots of jealous people spread rumors that I had paid off the judges. It was front-page news all over the country—it wasn't true, but nobody wanted to hear that. Because I was a young guy grabbing headlines in the boxing world, many jealous people saw this as a chance to knock me down a few rungs. Because Worldwide was beginning to make inroads in both basketball and football, all my competitors in those arenas who had powerful media contacts were quick to fuel the fire of controversy, hoping to make me look bad. I knew I did nothing wrong, and despite the weeks and weeks of controversy in the media (and even the intrusion of a private investigator), I was very content to enjoy Shannon's well-earned win. Eventually the furor died down because there was no substance to it. That's how it works when you're honest.

Being a successful person and having peace of mind at the same time is truly rare. You can have it if you choose to rise above the rest and always be ethical.

Be creative

Every day you're faced with basic business decisions. Throughout this book, I've tried to help you make those decisions—how to network, advertise, get motivated, work a room, and so on. I've shared many things that have worked for me, and I encourage you to give them a try. But don't stop there. Keep thinking. Be creative. Look at the decisions you routinely make without a second thought and ask yourself how you could reach the same goal through a different door— one that no one else has gone through. What can you do to be different from everybody else and improve your bottom line at the same time? Let me give you two examples of what I mean.

Right now I'm looking to hire an African-American male for the top position of CFO. (Many athletes I recruit are African-American. I think it's very important for me to have someone at the top who can relate to these young men and make them feel comfortable.) Hiring personnel is a pretty basic business practice. But I want the best and I don't want to use the usual channels that get me the usual people. I've been thinking about this move for a while and recently I saw an article in *The Wall Street Journal* that has given me a creative idea about how to find the right person. The article mentioned a professor at Harvard University who studies the rise of black executives. I'll bet this professor knows the most ambitious and productive black men in the country. I'm going to call him and ask for an introduction to some of these men. Why not? So many times, opportunities for contacts are right in front of us if we're willing to do things that are "out of the ordinary." Certainly, this professor is not in the employment business, but I can't imagine why he wouldn't want to help me and also give some up-and-coming young executives the opportunity of a lifetime. All I know is that it's worth a try. I always say to myself, "Why not?"

The second example illustrates a creative solution to an issue I face every day: I wanted a high-power broker to sell my company's stock. I thought I'd like to put the name Worldwide Entertainment and Sports right in front of him so he'd remember it. But I didn't want to do the usual thing of putting the company name on a pen, or notepad, or coffee mug. I wanted something really creative. Something big. So I thought: Big? Big? What's Big? And I came up with my answer: I sent the broker a 3' x 5' banner that said, "Steve Hamilton is the backbone of Worldwide." He laughed out loud and hung it up in his office. Now every day when he sits down at his desk, he stares at this *big* banner that keeps WWES on his mind.

Being unique requires courage—doing whatever it takes to meet a challenge that others wouldn't even try to overcome.

Think out of the box

Lots of people lose great opportunities to get publicity because they think too narrow. Then there are others who think wild and make it work.

Name recognition is key. To get that, you have to reach beyond the little world of your own industry. What we've done with boxer Shannon Briggs is a perfect example. We brought Shannon to a modeling agency (he's a naturally good-looking guy) and had him shot by the top photographers in the industry. Having these names behind his photos got him appearances in magazines like *Top Model* and *Vogue.* Then we got him to do runway shows for DKNY and Jockey. Then we went a step further and hooked him up with Shaquille O'Neal and he did some rapping with him and also on the Fugees album. These experiences got him coverage in music magazines like *Spin* and *Source.* Shannon's also a regular guest on the Howard Stern radio show. And he had a starring guest spot on the TV show *NY Undercover,* and has appeared on MTV. Now, Shannon's not just a boxer; he's a total entertainment entity.

I want to make sure that when one of my athletes does something not related to sports, that news is publicized. For example, not only is basketball rookie great Derek Anderson in *Slam Magazine* and *Sports Illustrated,* but we're expecting his face to be all over the place soon: We're hooking him up with rap music artist Master P, and he's in Spike Lee's movie, *He Got Game* with Denzel Washington. Any forum that will help you become a household name is a good one—use it.

The best stand out from the crowd. If you're doing what everybody else is doing to be successful, how can you expect to be more successful than they are?

Be different

If you're doing something that lots of other people are doing also, you've got to find a way to do it differently and make your work stand out. This was the position I was in when I was doing closed-circuit TV for boxing matches. It didn't matter what theater or arena people went to to see a match, they'd get the exact same evening at pretty much the same price anywhere. So I decided to make my shows different by bringing them to a whole different level than anyone had seen before. Instead of putting the shows in the usual sports arenas and movie theaters that attracted men in their old clothes and baseball caps, I wanted to make it an event with style. I moved it out of the theater and into a catering hall where I could give people a good dinner with music and an open bar. I knew people would pay a good dollar for a high-class night out that was just as good as being at the fight. I had people coming with dates, people coming all dressed up, people coming who had never seen a fight before. I had valet parking, raffles, appearances by celebrities and boxers. It was all first-class, top-notch. I also sold private rooms to corporations who brought their clients and friends. People had a great time, and I made a bundle. Suddenly my closed-circuit events were the talk of the town because they were different.

I also knew I wanted to do things my own way when I got into sports managing. From the start, that meant really caring about my athletes. I wanted them to have everything. I wanted to be there if they needed me. I wanted to know what was going on in their lives. But how could I realistically do that? For my boxers who weren't on the road with their teams, I decided to bring them into my house to live with me. I don't know of anybody else who's done that. Sure it was unique and different, but it was also practical. It made things work for me. It let me monitor their training, bond with them, watch out for their best interests. I don't do unique things just for the sake of being different. They have to make sense and get me to where I want to be.

Cultivate the ability to be different by following what you believe in. This will automatically set you apart from the crowd.

Make a scene

When you have a forum to make a big splash and draw attention to yourself, do it. Don't worry that no one else in the room is doing it too—that's what sets you apart. Remember the press conference announcing Shannon Briggs's upcoming fight with Lennox Lewis I told you about in the chapter about advertising? Take advantage of every opportunity to be recognized—and remembered.

Critical life lessons

- ✓ You don't have to make a spectacle of yourself to stand out in a crowd.

- ✓ If you want people to think you're special, make *them* feel special.

- ✓ You show how smart you are when you're honest enough to ask for help.

- ✓ It costs money to make money, so don't be afraid to spend what you don't have.

- ✓ Be persistent, relentless, and determined if you want to successfully separate yourself from the throngs of people who give up too soon.

- ✓ Choosing to be ethical allows you to stand out from the crowd.

- ✓ There's never one "right" way to do things. Be creative and find your own way.

- ✓ Tunnel vision keeps you from seeing the vast possibilities that are out there. If you want to be different from everyone else, don't get stuck in day-to-day ruts.

- ✓ Being unique doesn't mean being crazy. It means doing what works for you, regardless of what works for everybody else.

Be Reliable

The most important factor in determining success in your life is your reputation for reliability. If you say something like, "I'll get back to you tomorrow at 10," you have to make the call at 10, not 10:05. This makes all the difference in the world. To me, the worst trait in anybody—a friend, an employee, a client, anybody—is being unreliable.

The number-one asset I have is my reliability. If I say I'm going to do something, then I'm going to do it. If I tell you there'll be a car at the airport to meet you, it will be there. If I say I'm going to spend the weekend with one of my recruits, I'll do it; I won't send somebody else in at the last minute. I have to say that reliability has been the backbone of my success right from the start.

When I first asked Harvey Silverman to invest in my fledging company, I had to prove to him that I was a good investment—but how? I had nothing going for me—no money, no business history, no references, nothing—nothing except a keen willingness to be reliable. If I said I'd send him papers by a certain date, or would call at a certain time, or would bring certain information to a meeting, I *always* kept my word. If I invited him to a fight and said he would be in the front row—he was in the front row. A lot of times, even today, people tell me I'll be in the front row at something. I'll get there and I'll be in the third row. The third row is good, it's fine—but it's not the front row. If they had told me third row, I would have been happy. But don't say first and put me in third. Tell people like it is. You can blow a whole deal with something that small. You might figure, "What's the difference? First row? Third row?" The difference is in being true to your word. It's a lie when you're not.

An unreliable person is a dishonest person. If someone says she'll get back to you in an hour and you don't hear from her for two days, she lied to you.

Timing is everything

Being on time is not only the polite thing to do, it's a top business rule. You can't set up a meeting for 11 hoping you'll be back from your 10:30 meeting on time. You can't agree to go to an 11:30 conference across town knowing you have an office full of people coming in to see you at 11.

My feelings about being on time may be a genetic thing. I never met my great-grandfather, but everybody tells me he was notorious for being a stickler about promptness. If you said you were going to meet him at 10, he wouldn't wait past 10:01. My Uncle Allan also taught me a lot about being on time. He's not quite as impatient as my great-grandfather—he'll wait five minutes before he leaves. Like these other Roberts before me, unreliability drives me crazy.

People who are unreliable make my life more difficult. I set up a schedule based on what people tell me they're going to do. If they don't show up or if they're late or if they cancel, it throws off my whole day.

Reliability builds relationships

Being reliable is a great way to build loyal relationships within your company. If I say, "If you do this job for me without a hitch, you'll get a $3,000 bonus," I'll give that bonus without squabbling over any little snag. Even if it costs me up front, it's always to my advantage financially in the long run to let people know they can take me at my word.

It's also smart business sense to be considered reliable by the network of people you work so hard to build. A lot of times, people will ask me if I could introduce their friend, or client, or whoever to one of my athletes. Before I can pat a guy on the back with, "Oh, sure. Any time," I have to look over schedules and whatnot. Once I agree, I have an obligation to deliver. If I say you'll meet so-and-so—you will. That's another reason the people I work with are loyal to me. They're not going to disappoint somebody who never disappoints them. (See Rule #7 for more details on building loyalty.)

Of course, there are times you simply cannot keep your word. You might get stuck in traffic and miss a meeting. You might have a family emergency that keeps you from an important social event. Your cellular phone might not work. There are thousands of unforeseeable things that can happen to make you look unreliable. But that fact doesn't get you off the hook when it happens. You have to make sure that you take action to get yourself back into the good graces of the person you've disappointed. A simple, "I'm so sorry," won't do. Do something big, memorable, and sincere.

It is an ironic coincidence that in the middle of writing this chapter, I stood up my writer. We had an appointment to meet at my office at noon. On my way there, I found out that an important meeting in New York, that I thought was scheduled for 3 p.m., was really at 1:30 p.m. There was no way I could meet with my writer and make it to this meeting on time. Because she doesn't have a car phone or a beeper, it was too late to stop her trip all the way across the state (in the pouring rain), so I had to come up with a game plan to ease the blow. I know her son loves baseball (and I know her son is her soft spot), so I called Mike Mahone in merchandising and told him to come up with something that would make her trip worthwhile. She went home with two baseballs, one autographed by Ken Griffey, Jr., and the other by David Cone, feeling that her time wasn't completely wasted. When you can't come through, you've got to think quickly and do something to make up for it.

Not everyone is reliable

As you're building your reputation as a reliable person, don't expect everyone around you to be doing the same—not everyone is reliable. This isn't a complaint; it's a reality that you have to deal with if you want to keep your head above water. I learned this lesson very early in my career and I've remembered it every day since. It goes back to the days when I had just gotten into closed-circuit telecasts for big boxing matches. I got the rights in 1981 to show the first Sugar Ray Leonard vs. Tommy Hearns fight in a movie theater in New London, Conn. When I made the deal, I was told that there was no other closed-circuit location within 50 miles. I was really excited and was willing to pour a lot of money into the night because I felt I was guaranteed an automatic sellout with no competition in the area. I went up to New London two weeks before the fight to make sure everything was ready—I sent out flyers and ads, did radio spots, and all the things that make for a successful night. I went home feeling great. On my way to Las Vegas to see the fight, I decided to stop in New London again. When I got there, I found out that we had sold only 25 tickets! I also found out that there was a naval station in New London that had its own closed-circuit deal. This was obviously trouble. My first thought was to get out and promote like hell, but it was pouring rain—buckets of rain—and nobody was on the streets. All I had at that point was a theater with 1,700 empty seats. At the time of the fight, the weather cleared up, and believe it or not, we did sell out to a walk-up crowd. But even though I came out ahead, it was a harrowing experience that I never want to go through again—and I won't because now I know better than to take the word of any-one I don't know really well. I check everything out for myself way in advance.

Good credit signals a reliable person

I've always been conscientious about my credit. Since I was 19, I've had perfect TRWs, perfect TransUnions. I make sure there are no black marks on my record, because I think credit history is a reflection of reliability. If you don't have good credit, you've dug yourself into a hole that will keep many goals out of your reach. Don't think it won't hound you—in this electronic age, credit is just too easy to track. It's a neon indicator of your ability to be trusted. You've got to pay all your bills on time, because credit isn't just an indication of your financial state, it's an indication of your character.

My good credit record has been the foundation of my financial success. I couldn't have raised money on Wall Street to take the company public if I owed money all over the place, had defaulted on loans, or had established a history of late payments. No way. I couldn't have raised $3.5 million for my first deal or more than $12 million so far on my second deal if I had had five credit cards maxed to the limit. Your personal credit record is not personal. It's very much a measure of business ability.

I've paid back every penny I have ever borrowed, but it always surprises me when I make the payment and people say, "Ya know, you're the first person who has ever paid me back." How could you "borrow" money and walk away from the debt? Even if the person who gave you the loan doesn't hound you, that doesn't mean your future business life doesn't depend on your keeping your word to repay. There's just no way you can continue to do business with people you've scammed. They don't trust you anymore. They don't believe anything you say. If you say you're going to pay back money at a certain time or in certain installments—do it!

I speak from experience on this. In 1992, a childhood friend borrowed $2,700. When I gave him the money, I asked when he would pay it back. It could have been the next week, the next month, the next year. I didn't care. I just wanted a day. So he gave me a day— which passed about five years ago. A few months ago, he called and said he wanted to buy a house, but he needed $20,000. If he couldn't pay me back $2,700 in the last six years, why should I think he'd ever pay me back $20,000 now? If he had paid me back the smaller loan, I would have been glad to help him out again. But when someone doesn't pay me back, there are no more chances. The only upside of being stiffed is knowing that you'll never have to lend that person money again.

Because I believe so deeply that there is a relationship between a person's credit history and his or her ability to be reliable and dependable, I use the same criteria I hold myself to when I check out people who want to work with me. I'll run a credit check to find out what kind of people they are. If they can't keep their personal business in order, why would I trust them with mine?

People do check your credit history, so if you know there is a problem, bring it up before they get a report on it. Right up front explain any problems, give the circumstances, and make assurances that they are being rectified. This is far better than being rejected for a job based on a credit report that you've had no opportunity to defend yourself against.

Check your credit record every six months. Look for problems or errors and fix them before you enter into negotiations on a deal and don't have time to clean them up. You should also look into a service such as the TRW Credential Service that will notify you immediately if anything is ever filed on your credit record.

Business decisions based on reliability

Finding unreliable people is easy. Investors have told me, "You'll have the money tomorrow," then it never shows up. Stockbrokers have said, "I'll get behind your stock," but then they don't do it. These people are intentionally lying. This happens so often that I've come to assume everybody is unreliable until they prove me wrong. This is so important to me, I'll test people to gauge their level of reliability. It's simple; I don't even have to go out of my way to do it. I just say, "Get back to me tomorrow at 10 sharp," and then I see what happens. Or I'll say, "Send that by overnight mail so I have it tomorrow," or "Go to the library and get me 10 articles on this subject; I need them tomorrow." If I'm still waiting five days later, I've learned all I need to know. And I've learned it fast. I'd rather find out someone is unreliable in these types of circumstances than in the middle of an important business deal six months down the road. If you lose a major business deal because you were counting on somebody you've been working with for months and he or she doesn't come through, the blame is yours. You should have known way before the crucial moment that that person was unreliable.

We all have to prioritize who we're going to spend time with, who we're going to give our business to, who's on the top of our call-back list. The reliability factor helps me make these decisions. Once I'm sure somebody is reliable, he or she has my attention.

Reap the benefits of reliability

Do you want deals to go your way? Then be reliable. Let's say you get a set of contracts and you promise to look them over and make any changes by the end of the week. If you don't respond for two

---

weeks, every change you request will be a big deal. You will have put yourself in an adversarial position by being dishonest about what you were going to do. Things that might have been easily written in your favor at the end of that week will now become points of contention. Don't do this to yourself. If you need two weeks to do something—say so! But if you say two days, make it two days.

When I met with Donald Trump to work out the deal for the Briggs–Foreman fight, I promised him I'd personally bring a thousand people into the place. There were probably 50 other people vying for that fight telling him the same thing, but the word was out that if I say it, I do it. So Trump believed me. Making a promise like that might get me the fight, but if I then delivered only 100 people, he'd never want to deal with me again. That's not the kind of reputation I want to have. Reliability pays off in future dividends.

Do you want to make good deals with people with whom you network? Then be reliable. Mike Cantor, one of the wealthiest real estate developers in the country, was a guy I networked hard to meet. In the beginning, we didn't have the same philosophies, and I didn't know if just being honest and reliable was going to be enough to get him to work with me. But after eight years of doing one deal after another, always keeping my word, and always doing the right thing by him, he finally was ready to say, "I like your style. I'll work with you, no questions asked." Now we close deals on my word alone.

Reliability also has a reciprocal benefit. I know people keep their word to me because I've been so reliable in my dealings with them. Think about it: If you think nothing of keeping attorneys or brokers waiting three days for a piece of information, why should they keep their word to get right back to you? But if you're consistently true to your word, you'll find that people start noticing and will treat you the same way (most of the time).

Another benefit of knowing very reliable people is that I can recommend them to friends and business associates knowing they'll do an honest job. My friend Steve Goldstein is a perfect example. Steve used to manage real estate for me. Now he manages for my friends. The real estate business requires that people are honest because so much of it is a cash business. My partners always say, "Thank you so much for sending us Steve. He's so reliable and so loyal." Because they entrust Steve with so much responsibility (and often cash), they know he could rob them blind if he wanted to. But they know if I recommend him—they've got nothing to worry about.

If you want to deal with reliable people, show them through your own actions what that means.

The bottom line

As I look over the advice I've provided, I can see that reliability is the bottom line in almost every area of success. Think about it: In successful selling, networking, hiring, getting people motivated, negotiating, and so on, everything hinges on the way people perceive your credibility. Use that trait as a base on which you can build your success.

Critical life lessons

✓ Your level of reliability will determine your level of success.

✓ If you have nothing else going for you, prove yourself to be dependable and you'll eventually have it all.

✓ An unreliable person makes people doubt your credibility.

✓ Create some kind of reliability test before you invest too much time in any relationship.

✓ A person's credit history is an open book on the personal character trait of reliability.

✓ Every time you pay a bill on time, you're making an investment in your reputation.

✓ You can't count on other people to make you look reliable.

✓ Having the reputation of being a person of your word will open many business doors that otherwise would remain shut.

✓ Unreliable people are in the majority. Separate yourself from the crowd by keeping your word.

✓ Be honest about what you can and cannot do. It's far better to lose out on a deal because you were honest up front than to lose out after you've made promises you couldn't keep.

✓ Build your success on your reputation for being reliable and dependable.

Trust Your Gut

Successful businesspeople make important, life-changing decisions every day. To make these decisions, they gather facts and figures, they consult with experts, they check and recheck data. But in the end, they have to go with what their gut tells them is best. You have to be tuned into your natural instincts to know what's best for you. So if you want to play in the big league, you have to learn to trust your gut.

In each chapter of this book, I have offered business advice based on my own experiences. I've advised you to network, to surround yourself with successful people, to advertise, to stand out from the crowd, and so on. These are established tactics that you can read about and apply to your own situation to improve your chances of success in this very competitive world.

What I haven't yet mentioned is the role that instinct and natural inclinations play in making decisions about how and when and to what degree to do all these things. If an influential person is at the table across the room and appears standoffish, should you introduce yourself anyway? Your gut will tell you what's right. If you are interviewing candidates for a job (or being interviewed), after you have all the facts, it's your gut that you must rely on to make the best decision. When you are negotiating a contract and have to decide how much to give or take, it is your instincts and feelings that should be the determining factors. From the moment I left college against everyone's advice, to today when I make and break deals depending on how I "feel" about them, instinct has been my closest ally. I've learned that using too much of your head and not enough of your gut is a mistake.

Gut training

Your gut will be right more often than not if you give it two things:

1. **Information to work with.** It's not sound business advice to even say that you should make any decisions based solely on your first reaction. Even your gut needs the facts. Going with your gut does not mean jumping in with your eyes closed. It means taking the time to weigh the pros and cons, and to study the ramifications, strengths and weaknesses, facts and figures. Then, with all that in hand, it's time to step back and listen to what your instincts say about the deal. Sometimes everything looks perfect on paper, "the deal of a lifetime," but if something "feels" wrong, then you've got to turn it down. These instincts are not always right, but I've found that they're on target more often than not. That's why once I have all the facts in, I let my gut decide. If a deal feels bad, even though it looks good, I turn it down. If it feels great, even though the paperwork looks questionable, I go for it. Educate your gut to give you smart responses.

2. **Practice.** It's definitely true that the more you use your well-informed gut, the more often it will be right on target. At first, you may trust someone you shouldn't, but soon you'll learn from that. You might jump into exciting deals that don't have the backbone to stand up alone, but you get better at distinguishing between enthusiasm and instinct. You've heard the old expression: "Fool me once, shame on you. Fool me twice, shame on me." It's true. You have to be open to making mistakes when you make a judgment call based on strong feelings, but you also have to make sure you learn from those mistakes and don't let it happen again. Your gut is not infallible, but using it and exercising it will get it in shape for top performance.

It's a big mistake if you decide not to ever trust your gut again if it burns you. It's a sign that you should use it more often.

Judging character

I'm a very good judge of character. I can just feel when someone is not to be trusted. I can tell when someone is telling it straight. This is an instinctive call, but it's usually based on careful observation. I watch body language for signals: What kind of handshake does he have? Does she make eye contact? Does he sit far away or up close? Then I pay attention to things such as dress and grooming. Is she neat? Is he well-dressed? Are the nails and teeth clean? I tune into speech patterns. Does she speak clearly? Does he mumble? This all comes together to give me a gut reaction that is very seldom wrong. I look at someone and try to envision him being successful. I ask myself if I believe he'll do what he says he'll do. I have to ask myself if I can rely on this person. There's no one thing that will give me a positive answer; it's a collection of things that come together giving my sense of judgment what it needs to make a sound decision.

This is especially important when you're in a people business. When I'm recruiting young athletes, I get very thorough scouting reports that tell me career stats. I know who's the best and who I want to go after. But I won't make a final decision on anybody until I've had time to meet him and get a feeling about the kind of person he is. I can tell right away if he's someone who will be loyal to me or if he'll leave me as soon as another agent waves something big under his nose. This information isn't on any scouting report. I have to feel this out for myself by spending some time with the athlete and letting my gut decide.

Being a good judge of character also helps me make good investment decisions. I've had experiences where I've wanted to invest in private placements in the stock market. On paper, the companies looked worthless, but knowing that the people behind them were good, hard-working people let me feel positive about the future potential of the company. Just looking at the specs, you'd say I was nuts to put my money on the line. But I wasn't making the decision based on paperwork; I was putting my trust in people. You have to have a strong inner feeling about someone to do that. And the reverse is true, too. People have brought me investment opportunities that looked great on paper. It looked like something I couldn't possibly lose on. But then I'd meet the people behind it and decide that it just wasn't for me. Something inside me wasn't satisfied. You've got to meet the people you invest in; there's no away around it. I've learned this the hard way. I invested in a company that was supposed to present the latest in Internet encryption. Along with a strong group of very wealthy people, I put in $200,000. It turned out that the people behind the company were the best in computer know-how, but were the worst in business smarts. They let the market get away from them and had to sell the company for peanuts. If I had met these people, I would have been able to see right away that they couldn't compete; I have no doubt that I would have known they lacked the business sense to make the company fly. Instead, I listened to everyone else and went ahead without a personal meeting. Big mistake.

Your gut also should be allowed to enter into your negotiations. When someone puts a number on the table, you have to instinctively make a decision if it's the real number or if it's just a ploy. Like in poker, you have to know who's bluffing if you want to win the game. When I was negotiating the Foreman–Briggs fight, I thought a very low figure was put on the table. I knew Foreman wanted the fight with Shannon, so I had to use that feeling to make a decision. My gut said to hold out for the big numbers. I put myself in their position and felt that, in their shoes, I wouldn't let this deal go. I had only my gut to help me do that.

Good business is all about being able to decipher who's real and who's not.

Throwing caution to the wind

Some people say it's good business practice to take things slowly, weigh everything carefully, and approach all situations and opportunities with caution. This is good advice—to a point. You want to use all available resources to gather information. But once you've done that, you either go or you don't. You have to ask yourself, "Why should I be cautious if I really believe in this?" If you have a clear vision of where you're going, go for it. But if you hesitate, you're defeated before you start. At some point, you have to block out facts, figures, and other people's opinions, and ask yourself, "How do *I* feel about this?"

If the answer is "scared," that's okay—use that fear to your advantage. Either turn it into adrenaline to push you forward, or listen to it as a warning that this is not right for you. But use your feelings to get yourself off the fence. If you back down, you're free to go after something else. If you go forward, you've got direction and purpose. If you sit there, you're useless to yourself.

In the early 80s, I was in Plainfield working with my fighters when I met a trainer named John Davenport. He invited me to go with him one day to watch Tommy Hearns in a charity exhibition fight. John was a personal friend of Hearns's trainer and manager, Emanuel Steward, and I had a feeling this was going to be good for business. Sure enough, after the fight, John took me into the locker room and I met Tommy Hearns and his manager and trainer. This was another one of those once-in-a-lifetime opportunities that I just couldn't resist jumping into, because my gut told me I couldn't miss the chance to make something happen. Forget being cautious.

"Nice to meet you," I said. "I'm from Madison Avenue. Advertising and athletes are my specialties. How come you don't have endorsements? You're leaving a lot of money on the table if you don't get yourself into advertising." I have to confess, at that point I don't think I had ever actually been in a building on Madison Avenue. But I convinced these guys that I was an expert, and the next thing I knew, I was flying out to Detroit to sign a deal to secure product endorsements for the upcoming Hearns vs. Sugar Ray Leonard fight.

My gut told me this was a great opportunity; my head told me I didn't know a thing about it. It didn't matter now, I was off! I spent the next six months flying all over the country at my own expense to get Hearns endorsement deals with big-name companies like McGregor and Goodyear. Eventually I had put together a $1.5-million package (that would be about $100,000 for me!). There was just one catch. Each contract had the same stipulation: Hearns had to win the fight to get the endorsement deal. This didn't sound like a problem to an optimistic guy like me.

Today's fights are about 12 rounds, but in those days, they were 15. After the 12th round, Hearns was the hands-down winner; the only way he could lose was if he got knocked out. At that point, I was counting my money and planning my next move to get more athletes and more endorsements. This fight was going to launch a new division of my business.

Then in the 14th round, Leonard lunged out like a bull and knocked Hearns clear through the ropes—he was out cold.

So how does this show that going with your gut is a good idea? Well, actually a lot of good came out of this. I did get myself in the position to sell endorsements. I had convinced the Hearns team to hire me and then I convinced major companies to give me $1.5 million. If I had done it once, I knew I could do it again. And another positive was that I had learned a lot about this side of the business. I had to figure that at a time when I was supposed to still be in college, I was getting hands-on experience and making deals for Tommy Hearns; this was stuff a college kid could only dream about. In addition to all this, because of my connection with Tommy Hearns, his people got me the rights to run closed-circuit fights in a theater in New London, Conn. This was a nice consolation; even though I lost the big score when Hearns went down, I made a little bit of money promoting the fight through pay-per-view and I learned enough to make it a very lucrative side business down the road. And the biggest plus of the whole situation was that I became close to Hearns's trainer, Emanuel Steward, who taught me so much about this business. He became an invaluable mentor. By my count, even though the endorsement deals never actually went through, I was still way ahead of the game. I hadn't lost a thing.

I used the same "jump now, look later" approach when Bob Arum asked me if I'd like to manage three of the 1988 Olympic boxers, including the gold medalist, Ray Mercer. Bob felt I had paid my dues and was now ready for prime time. There was no question that this was my big break. I didn't even have to go to the Olympics in Korea to sign them; Arum was ready to just hand them to me. So I jumped on it and told him that I had already lined up the million dollars needed to manage these guys. The truth is: I had nothing, but I knew deep down that I could do it and nothing was going to stop me. It was a challenge and I was focused and relentless. I wasn't going to hesitate and ask Arum to wait to see if I could scrape it together. I would do it, no doubt about it—no need for caution or hesitation. When you see something good, you sign and figure out the details later. This is the kind of situation where you have to let your beliefs, your vision, and

your insides speak for you. Once your goals and your vision are secure, there's no need to hesitate when you see an opportunity that will
help you make them a reality.

Get the deal now. Figure out how you'll work it later.

Following your own drummer

Sometimes your gut will push you in a direction that everyone will
tell you is wrong. But because they don't have *your* instincts about
what's right for *you*, who are you going to listen to? I really had to ignore everybody around me when I decided to leave college: "You'll
never amount to anything now," they told me. I had to ignore everyone when I decided to take Triple Threat public: "You're dreaming.
Nobody takes boxers public," they insisted. (Taking three fighters
public sounded nuts even to me, but I just knew deep down that it
was the right move to make.) I really heard it when I decided to manage Ray Mercer again after he had gone with another manager in the
Triple Threat takeover. "He burned you once, he'll burn you again,"
everyone told me. "He's down and out now. Why would you put your
time into somebody like that?" they all asked. But I knew that lots of
the things that had happened weren't Ray's fault. I felt he had been
badly influenced by his trainer. I knew he had lost confidence and
picked up bad habits. I had this feeling that I had a lot to prove; it
was a challenge. My gut told me to accept the challenge because I had
everything to gain and nothing to lose. Everyone thought he was finished anyway, so if nothing happened, no one would be surprised. If I
turned his career around, I'd be a hero. Anytime I have an opportunity where I can't lose, my insides tell me to jump at it no matter
what everybody else thinks.

In all these instances (and in many, many others), people told me
I was an idiot. From their point of view, each move looked like a bad
one. But what if I had let other people make my decisions for me? I
certainly wouldn't have been the first sports agent to take a company
public. I wouldn't have been successful in a very cut-throat, competitive field. And I sure wouldn't have been in a position to offer you any
advice. People always ask me, "How did you know these things could

possibly work out?" The only answer that makes any sense is, "I felt it in my bones. The feeling was so strong, I just couldn't turn away."

The people around you only see things in black-and-white. They don't see your vision. They don't know what drives you. They don't know anything about your level of commitment. They don't know your burning desire to succeed. They don't know the sacrifices you're willing to make to reach your goal. Only you know these things. Only you can make the right decision for you.

Critical life lessons

- ✓ When all the facts are in and you've listened to everyone's advice, only you know what feels right.

- ✓ A gut reaction is not irresponsible. It's a response from deep down inside based on all your life experiences. You have to learn to hear it and respect it.

- ✓ Give your gut information to work with and then exercise it over and over. If it makes a mistake, learn from the mistake and then give your gut another try.

- ✓ Being a good judge of character comes from natural instincts. This will serve you well in all business ventures.

- ✓ When you make a decision that will affect *your* life, don't make the one that will please other people more than it pleases you.

- ✓ Those who hesitate when the stakes are really high will never know what it's like to fly without a net.

- ✓ Understand the sacrifice it will take to make a commitment, stop at nothing to achieve it, and go for it.

- ✓ When the decision is a big one, gather the facts, seek advice, and then tune in to your feelings. They have to have a say in the decision-making process.

Give Back

I feel very fortunate with what I have and I'm always aware that I've been blessed. This awareness pushes me to give to others who haven't been so lucky. Although I don't expect anything back business-wise from what I give, to tell you the truth, I do trust the belief that God is keeping track and will reward me in the end.

The concept of "balance" is very important in success. I've talked about balancing the good with the bad, the failures with the successes, the ups with the downs. It's also important to balance what you take with what you give. As you're working your way to the top, be sure to look around and show some social responsibility for the world you live in.

Give back through charities

The most obvious way a successful person can give back to society is through contributions to charities. My favorite charity is Project Pride in Newark, N.J. This is an organization that works with kids from kindergarten to college. I was born in Newark and I've been known for years to be a champion of the kids there. Project Pride supports education, recreation, and college scholarships. Each year, it sponsors about 6,000 kids in its recreational athletic program. The charity sponsors an SAT (Scholastic Aptitude Test) program with an 85-percent college-placement record. It has a reading-enrichment program that has helped 5,000 kids improve their reading skills. This year, it will give out $102,000 in college scholarships. These are all things that I personally think are very important for inner-city kids. These kids are going to grow up and either contribute positively to society or bring it down. I'd like to think I had a hand in giving them something to reach for. I also like the way Project Pride is organized. With many other charities, you don't know how much of your donation is actually going to the cause. But Project Pride gives about 97 cents of every dollar to the kids. There is no full-time staff, there is no executive director, there's no telephone, and except for the reading teachers, all staff members are volunteers. That's my kind of charity.

Part of the big picture of success asks you to not be so absorbed in yourself that you forget to help other people.

Giving back doesn't have to wait until you've made it to the top. It's a personal and business practice that should be a part of who you are. It shows your willingness to work hard and share the good things you gain with those less fortunate. This doesn't mean you have to give only with your checkbook; there are lots of other ways to give to charitable organizations. Be creative. You can volunteer your time. (I bring my athletes to charity events to attract attention to the cause and raise money.) You can sponsor some kind of fund raiser at company events. (When I wanted to get Lennox Lewis to fight Mercer again, I offered him $20 million and challenged him to donate half of his winnings to Project Pride if he lost.) You can donate items for charity auctions. (We always send signed sports memorabilia to charity auctions all over the country.) You can support fund raisers. You can offer to take part in walks, marathons, and street fairs. You can donate used office equipment or computers. The possibilities are endless—so there are no acceptable excuses.

How can you enjoy your own success if you're not tuned into the rest of the world and the needs of others?

Some people may criticize your charity work as self-serving. I won't deny that giving to charity is also a great way to get publicity and to make contacts, but that goes with the territory. In another instance, before the 1997 NBA draft, number-one picks Derek Anderson and Bobby Jackson went to a playground in Harlem, N.Y., to meet with the neighborhood kids. We made sure they got good press for their charity work. The action was from their hearts—the result was on the front page. I don't think there's anything wrong with that. The kids in Harlem sure weren't complaining. Bobby and Derek felt good, and the press was happy. It's often a win-win situation.

There is also a fear out there that if you give to a charity, the people associated with that charity are in your debt, creating a conflict of interest. That's garbage, but it happens. Recently, I sold off some stock and I donated $138,000 to my favorite charity. But because someone involved in the sports industry is on the board of this charity, the donation was promptly returned. When this happens, it's very aggravating because it reflects on your integrity and your motives. But don't get crazy and swear off all charities. In this case, an Easter Seals camp in Alabama for physically challenged children was very happy to take the donation instead. In fact, it was the largest single donation the camp had ever received. Their letter thanking me for the donation appears on the next page.

Give back to your friends

A good, solid friendship has to have a give-back foundation. Too often, so-called "friendships" hinge on "what have you done for me today?" But for me to consider myself successful in life, I need to know that I have friends who know I value them as people and treasure their companionship more than their wallets.

Michael Cantor and Jim Nuckle are two very good friends of mine who are perfect examples of what I mean by a "give-back" relationship. Both of them have told me that because they're worth more than a hundred million dollars, people always have their hands out everywhere they turn. People want to meet them so they can ask for a loan or use them in some other way. To this day, I make sure I'm always giving friends like Mike and Jim things to show my commitment to our friendship. Along with my time and attention, I give them stock advice, tickets to sporting events, a good time at restaurants and nightclubs, valuable business contacts, and more, whenever I can.

Helping people be successful in their business is a powerful way to contribute to a friendship. When you're out networking for your own gain, consider how your networking can help others, too. I like to

Roberts Rules!

ALABAMA'S SPECIAL CAMP FOR CHILDREN AND ADULTS

CAMP ASCCA — EASTER SEALS
P.O. BOX 21 • JACKSON GAP, AL 36861
205/825-9226 • 1-800-843-2267 (ALABAMA ONLY)

JERRY BYNUM, ADMINISTRATOR

April 23, 1998

Marc Roberts

Dear Marc:

On behalf of the campers, volunteers and staff of Camp ASCCA-Easter Seals, thank you for your very generous donation. We are delighted that you have chosen Camp ASCCA-Easter Seals as the recipient of your philanthropy and we can assure you that your gift will help make the lives brighter for the thousands of campers with disabilities that participate at Camp ASCCA-Easter Seals each year.

Camp ASCCA-Easter Seals is the largest camp for people with disabilities in the world. Situated on 230 acres along Alabama's largest recreational lake, Camp ASCCA-Easter Seals is a $10 million recreational and educational center that provides traditional and innovative camp activities to children and adults with disabilities, offering activities such as sports, fishing, canoeing, crafts, swimming, horseback riding and ropes course activities.

You will be pleased to know that your gift is the largest single donation that we have received from an individual contributor in our 22-year history. Your contribution comes at a particularly exciting time, in that we have just launched a campaign to raise $3 million in endowment funds over the next 10 years.

Enclosed are some Camp ASCCA-Easter Seals promotional items to welcome you to our camp family. However, the best way we can show our appreciation is to invite you to visit camp and see first-hand the value of your contribution. One look at the smiling faces of our campers will convince you that you have made a gift that will significantly enhance the lives of thousands of children for years to come.

Although programs run at camp year-round, our summer sessions officially begin June 1. We would be happy to accommodate your schedule in any way, however we might suggest scheduling a visit sometime during the week of June 28-July 3, which is our Sports Camp for children with disabilities. Let us know when you would like to visit and we will make travel arrangements for yourself and Peter.

Marc, thanks for choosing Camp ASCCA-Easter Seals to benefit from your good will. We look forward to meeting you and proudly showing you Camp ASCCA-Easter Seals.

Sincerely,

Glenn Roswal
Chair, Board of Directors

Jerry Bynum
Administrator

Shannon Gooden
Director of Development

bring lots of people together and let them meet each other and create their own synergies. If there are 10 people in the room, I'll promote each person to the other nine as if I were his or her personal PR agent. Always using the superlative, I'll say: "This guy is the best investment banker." "Meet the best retailer in sports merchandising." "I want you to meet the top lawyer in the country." I'll do this all night and never say a word about myself. I make sure entrepreneurs meet investors, and people in real estate meet bankers, and stockbrokers meet lawyers. Now, each of the 10 people have met nine other people with whom they can network. Many times this leads to big business deals and lasting friendships. When these people make good, solid contacts through me, it generates a lot of good will and sometimes a big commission.

Give back to your neighborhood

When you make it big, don't forget where you came from. I think a person's willingness to look back and remember the people back home is a strong indicator of character.

I've never forgotten where I was born: Newark, N.J. Today, this is a place where young people are lost, thrown away, or locked up. I have something that I know can help. Ten years ago, I brought in the Triple Threat. Boxers Charles Murray, Ice Cole, and Ray Mercer became role models who the kids could relate to. This was the biggest thing that happened to that city since the old days of boxing when Friday-night TV covered Newark boxing matches. I built my gym, I brought city kids in to watch and talk to my fighters, I promoted fights with big-name boxers, and gave kids a place to go and something to reach for. (Remember that boxing is the only sport in which the athletes have to pass drug tests after every fight.) Even today, I'm the only one bringing top-notch boxing to Newark. I'll take Shannon Briggs and Ray Mercer from their fights in Atlantic City to ones in Newark. When I do this I lose money because there are no corporate sponsors. But there's more to being successful than always looking for money—or even notoriety.

Giving back to your old neighborhood won't necessarily get you a pat on the back, but that doesn't mean it's not worthwhile. I don't get much press, recognition, or thanks for what I do in Newark. In fact, sometimes I get the boot. Recently, I was at an opening of a new boxing gym where politicians were out in their re-election year glory. I told the executive director of the gym that I'd like to speak to the crowd and donate $2,500 to the program. He never introduced me. I can't say why; I can only guess that maybe there were egos on the platform who didn't want to share the credit that day. Who knows? But it does point out that not everyone is going to be grateful when you try to give back. Don't let that stop you from trying.

Give back to business associates

The expression, "One hand washes the other," is a statement of fact: Each hand needs the other to get the job done. I need things other people can give me, and they need things I can give them. That includes money, contacts, information, and the like. If somebody does me a favor, I do one for her. In fact, I never forget it and I always repay it tenfold. That's how things work in successful business relationships.

I've held to this philosophy right from the start. When I started doing my boxing events in Newark, for example, a lot of people were jealous and saying bad things about me just because I was young. But there was a promoter named Gabe Laconte who was very supportive of me. He appreciated the hard work I did. And he defended me to anyone who tried to spread more lies. Because Gabe was loyal to me and always wanted good things for me, I considered that a great favor. I don't forget that kind of person and I'm quick to give back. I'll do anything for Gabe now. When I bring my fighters into Newark, only Gabe does the promotions.

When somebody helps you, don't forget it. Repaying favors is also a way to keep yourself from being indebted to anybody. That's good business sense. Always try to give more than you take.

Critical life lessons

✓ Giving back isn't something reserved for the very rich or for your spare time. It should be an integral part of your life right now.

✓ Find a charity you believe in and you'll feel good deep down every time you lend them a hand.

✓ Charitable organizations don't need only your money; they're glad to have your time, your skills, and your attention.

✓ Charitable work and contributions are not always recognized and rewarded. Give anyway.

✓ A give-back philosophy is the foundation of solid, long-lasting friendships.

✓ Let your friends benefit from your business relationships by introducing others' friends and clients for their own networking purposes.

✓ Never forget your roots.

✓ Accept a favor only if you're willing to pay it back tenfold.

✓ The habit of giving keeps you from ever being indebted.

Client List

NFL Players

Antonio Freeman—Green Bay Packers
Tyrone Drakeford—New Orleans Saints
O.J. McDuffie—Miami Dolphins
Tyrone Wheatley—New York Giants
Bobby Engram—Chicago Bears
Brentson Buckner—Cincinnati Bengals
Spencer George—Houston Oilers
Willie Jackson—Jacksonville Jaguars
Larry Shannon—Miami Dolphins
Brad Baxter—Detroit Lions
Charles Johnson—Pittsburgh Steelers
Ray Zellars—New Orleans Saints
Karl Hankton—Philadelphia Eagles
Tony Hutson—Dallas Cowboys
Stephen Davis—Washington Redskins
Rickey Dudley—Oakland Raiders
Sean Hill—Detroit Lions
Corey Sawyer—Cincinnati Bengals
Jamal Fountaine—Atlanta Falcons
Antonio London—Detroit Lions
Frankie Smith—San Francisco 49ers
William Gaines—Washington Redskins
Victor Riley—Kansas City Chiefs
Herman O'Berry—Free agent
Jason Chorak—St. Louis Rams

Roberts Rules!

Tony Parrish—Chicago Bears
Antuwane Ponds—Washington Redskins
Vashon Adams—Kansas City Chiefs
Lance Johnstone—Oakland Raiders

NBA/European Players

Bobby Jackson—Denver Nuggets
Johnny Newman—Denver Nuggets
Derek Anderson—Cleveland Cavaliers
Jason Osborne—US Representation
Walter Berry—US Representation
Alvin Sims—Quad City Thunder
Shawnelle Scott—Cleveland Cavaliers
Kebu Stewart—Philadelphia 76ers
Antonio Watson—US Representation

World Champion Boxers

"Merciless" Ray Mercer—Heavyweight
Shannon Briggs—Heavyweight
Tracy Patterson—Lightweight
Danell Nicholson—Heavyweight
Charles "The Natural" Murray—Junior Welterweight
Alex Trujillo—Lightweight

Marketing Clients

Kevin Delaney—Snowboarding
Brian Delaney—Snowboarding
Casey Atwood—LAR Motorsports

Index

Risking money on publicity, 118-119
Risks, taking, 17-20, 24, 31, 33
  with money, 211-212
Roberti, Todd, 192
Rodman, Dennis, 119
Rubenstein, Rich, 176
Rudolph, Erik, 158

Sacrificing, 20, 106-107
Sale, packaging, 28-29
Sales pitch, how to give, 125-136
Sampson, Ralph, 101
Scharf, Gary, 72, 151
Schinman, Ryan, 50, 64, 158
Schneider, John, 175
Segal, Joel, 49, 72, 80, 150
Selling a dream, 31-32
Selling yourself, 27-32
Seminars, attending, 143-144
Sierra, Ruben, 101
Signed agreement,
  importance of, 38
Silverman, Harvey, 47-48, 128,
  140, 210, 219
Socializing, 171-194
Spear, Leeds & Kellogg, 47, 128, 140
Stallone, Sylvester, 200-201
Starling, Marlin, 196
Staying focused, 97-108
Steinbrenner, George, 179
Stern, Howard, 103, 119, 215
Steward, Emanuel, 187, 233-234
Stockholders, making employees, 77
Strength, 40-41
  in negotiating, 161-162
Success, following, 137-145

Taking a company public, 27-32,
  39-40, 97-98
Television, 112-114
Temporary employees, 59-60
Thinking creatively, 114
Thoroughness, 130
Throwing caution to
  the wind, 232-235
Time, wasting in
  negotiations, 166-167
Timing, 220
Tolerito, Vito, 21
Tools, giving employees
  the right, 77-78
TOPjobs USA, 63
Training, gut, 230
Trial and error, 33
Trouble, dealing with, 33-42
Trump, Donald, 46, 101, 225
Trusting your gut, 229-236
Tyson, Mike, 101, 151

Unique, being, 209-217

Verbal commitment, 38
Videotapes, 111-112

Walker, Samaki, 118-119
Washington, Denzel, 215
Wheatley, Tyrone, 80, 90, 127
Williamson, John "Up-the-Ladder,"
  38-39
Wilson, Darroll, 40, 152
Working a room, 171-184

Ziering, Peter, 104